P9-DWE-833

ANTIDEMOCRACY IN AMERICA

Public Books Series

Sharon Marcus and Caitlin Zaloom, Editors

Founded in 2012, *Public Books* is required reading for anyone interested in what scholars have to say about contemporary culture, politics, and society. The monographs, anthologies, surveys, and experimental formats featured in this series translate the online experience of intellectual creativity and community into the physical world of print. Through writing that exemplifies the magazine's commitment to expertise, accessibility, and diversity, the Public Books Series aims to break down barriers between the academy and the public in order to make the life of the mind a public good.

Think in Public: A Public Books Reader, edited by Sharon Marcus and Caitlin Zaloom, 2019

Antidemocracy in America: Truth, Power, and the Republic at Risk, edited by Eric Klinenberg, Caitlin Zaloom, and Sharon Marcus, 2019

ANTIDEMOCRACY IN AMERICA

TRUTH, POWER, AND THE REPUBLIC AT RISK

Edited by

ERIC KLINENBERG
CAITLIN ZALOOM
SHARON MARCUS

COLUMBIA UNIVERSITY PRESS
NEW YORK

Columbia University Press
Publishers Since 1893
New York   Chichester, West Sussex
cup.columbia.edu
Copyright © 2019 Eric Klinenberg, Caitlin Zaloom, and Sharon Marcus
All rights reserved

Library of Congress Cataloging-in-Publication Data
Names: Klinenberg, Eric, editor. | Zaloom, Caitlin, editor. | Marcus,
    Sharon, 1966– editor.
Title: Antidemocracy in America : truth, power, and the republic at risk /
    edited by Eric Klinenberg, Caitlin Zaloom, and Sharon Marcus.
Description: New York : Columbia University Press, [2019] | Series: Public
    books series | Includes bibliographical references.
Identifiers: LCCN 2018061396 (print) | LCCN 2019002481 (ebook) |
    ISBN 9780231548724 (e-book) | ISBN 9780231190107 (cloth : alk. paper) |
    ISBN 9780231190114 (pbk. : alk. paper)
Subjects: LCSH: United States—Politics and government—2017– |
    Conservatism—United States—History—21st century. | Trump, Donald,
    1946– | Political culture—United States—21st century.
Classification: LCC E912 (ebook) | LCC E912 .A58 2019 (print) |
    DDC 306.20973/0905—dc23
LC record available at https://lccn.loc.gov/2018061396

♾

Columbia University Press books are printed on permanent and durable
acid-free paper.
Printed in the United States of America

Cover design: Julia Kushnirsky
Cover photo: Ted Eytan, MD
Book design: Lisa Hamm

CONTENTS

PART II. THE COLLAPSE: HOW WE GOT HERE

PART III. THE SOLUTIONS: WHAT WE CAN DO

ANTIDEMOCRACY IN AMERICA

INTRODUCTION: THE BIG PICTURE

ERIC KLINENBERG

This book, which I edited with Sharon Marcus and Caitlin Zaloom of *Public Books*, is a collective effort to assess the presidency of Donald Trump and the effects of America's unsettling turn toward authoritarian rule. It's a call for us to pull back from the deluge of tweets and breaking news stories that turn each day into a political drama, to consider the big picture that's slowly emerging from the dark places we inhabit today.

How did we get here? Decades of economic stagnation and rising inequality have rekindled support for antidemocratic political parties throughout the developed world. Nativism, ethnonationalism, and the misogyny and homophobia that accompany them have fueled the campaigns. In recent years, European nations have harbored and succumbed to authoritarian movements. And on November 8, 2016, citizens of the world's strongest democratic nation elected a reality-television star and real-estate tycoon with no previous governing experience to be their president. It was, by any stretch of the imagination, an extraordinary leap into the unknown for America and, by virtue of its hyperpower status, for the rest of the world.

The articles in this book, written by many of the nation's leading social scientists and humanists, leverage the power of scholarly knowledge to explore the causes, consequences, and meanings of this dark turn. They also point to ways forward. But the essays—including this one, which Sharon and Caitlin contributed to and shaped—are motivated by a set of recent events that are worth cataloguing so that we can establish the context for our inquiry.

Donald Trump launched his political career by questioning the citizenship of the nation's first African American president, Barack Obama. He campaigned for office by promising to enact policies antithetical to open societies: curbing civil rights and liberties, including free speech; building a massive southern border wall; limiting the franchise; imprisoning reporters; reducing oversight of police violence and the criminal-justice system; and allying with dictators and thugs. He was aggressively nativist, impugning the character of Mexicans and Arabs and denigrating Jews and blacks. He was unapologetically misogynist, for gun rights, and against reproductive rights. He led rallies where he encouraged supporters to physically injure his political opponents. Trump's supporters chanted: "Build a wall!" and "Lock her up!"

Trump demeaned government and the professional public servants who work for it. He pledged to blow up the system: terminating trade agreements and climate treaties, pulling back from international diplomacy, putting "America first." He denied the validity of established science, particularly on climate change. He said he'd revive the moribund coal industry, return factories to the rust belt, let oil companies drill in the oceans, and rebuild a massive fossil-fuel pipeline that his predecessor had rejected. He promised to protect—even expand—the rights of gun owners and to roll back the rights of women to control their own bodies and lives.

Like Bernie Sanders, the surprisingly popular socialist candidate who nearly won the Democratic nomination, Trump claimed to champion those left behind by globalization, deindustrialization, and the financial economy. Unlike Sanders, though, Trump welded his populist message to an exclusionary, racist one, galvanizing the alt-right and other openly bigoted forces previously on the fringe of American life. What's more, he did it dishonestly, by promising to restore a past that can never return—not least because it never existed in the first place.

We went for it. Not all of us. Not even most of us. But you don't get into the White House by winning the popular vote. You get there by winning the Electoral College, and Trump did, by a commanding margin. In January 2017, he became the nation's forty-fifth president. Americans, including many who voted for him, braced for the storm Trump would bring.

In office, as in the electoral campaign, President Trump has repeatedly attacked sacred Enlightenment projects, including science, journalism, and the relentless pursuit of truth. He has propagated misinformation. He has complimented and cozied up to despots across the planet, including Vladmir Putin and Recep Tayyip Erdogan, and has insulted leaders of open democratic societies with whom the United States has long been allied. Trump has advocated slashing public support for medical research, climate science, laboratory science, social science, the humanities, and the arts. He has ordered that vital research on health, the environment, and security be halted or revised. He has demanded that important public data be discarded and erased.

Trump is opposed to public knowledge and intellectual freedom. He demands strict loyalty and is against transparency. He has fired intelligence officials who have investigated his administration and his businesses. He has threatened media companies that dig for information that he'd prefer to keep buried, labeled journalists "the lowest form of life" and "enemies of the people," and—in true authoritarian fashion—called for the termination of a reporter (one of many, but the most prominent female African American) who called him a "white supremacist."

He has established himself, his cabinet, and the government he leads as adversaries of reason.

Trump failed to take a strong moral stand against the extreme right as it has marched across the country, even after Charlottesville, when a white supremacist committed homicidal terrorism. He began dismantling Obamacare and made health insurance less affordable for millions of people. He neglected to mobilize national resources that could have helped nearly two million American citizens who'd lost access to drinking water and electricity after Hurricane Maria, and he insulted Puerto Rican political leaders who called for help as thousands of their neighbors were suffering and dying out of most Americans' sight.

Trump's malign neglect of vulnerable American citizens in postdisaster situations has been less visible than his ruthless acts of violence against those who come to the United States seeking refuge or opportunity, particularly those without official documentation. His administration has detained and then separated immigrant families, effectively kidnapping thousands of infants and children, hundreds of whom may never see their families again. Amnesty International and legal scholars around the world have called this cruel policy "nothing short of torture." In some cases, the policy has resulted in child deaths.

At the time of this writing, in early 2019, the government is shut down because of Trump's insistence that Congress fund a multibillion-dollar wall along the southern border. The nation is bracing for Trump's reaction to Special Counsel Robert Mueller's report, as well as the possibility that Trump will demand Mueller's termination. It's not yet clear where the moral bottom is nor how adversarial to reason, repressive of dissent, and vindictive against those he despises the president will ultimately manage to be.

There are some who claim that strong laws and institutions will sustain American civil society and uphold our democratic system no matter how aggressively the Trump administration tries to upend them. It's possible, but Western history suggests that important social institutions, including religious organizations, journalism, the academy, and even the courts, can quickly fold beneath the pressure of a vindictive autocrat and his henchmen—particularly if the nation is at war with a foreign power or if a minority group is proclaimed an "enemy within."

Today, at least, the demise of our major civic and legal institutions may seem unlikely. Most Americans disapprove of the president's performance. The special counsel is methodically examining the recent behavior of Trump's family, business, administration, and campaign staff. The Department of Justice has already indicted several former members of the Trump campaign team and a number of Russian agents. Prominent Trump associates, including his attorney, Michael Cohen, and his campaign chairman, Paul Manafort, have been convicted of crimes and sentenced to prison. Social movements are resurgent. There are protests everywhere.

Yet it's hard to be confident that this organized resistance can combat the assault on our democratic institutions. The Republican Party has become an instrument of the Trump administration, and an overwhelming majority of Republicans in Congress has supported even the most extreme of Trump's policy ideas. A war may be imminent, potentially one involving nuclear weapons that could reach America's shores and cities. Mass deportation of undocumented immigrants, as well as the hundreds of thousands granted "temporary protected status" and living here legally over the past decades, remains possible.

No one knows which people and institutions will become Trump's next targets, or whether his party and cabinet will support his brazen acts. Trump is vain, thin-skinned, and unforgiving. He invents history. He fabricates social facts. His list of enemies is long and growing. And, as Americans learned while watching him boast about grabbing pussies, evade tax payments, fleece students, and refuse to pay his contractors: Trump is ruthless. Whatever he can get away with, he will.

Why do we need a scholarly perspective on a current situation that already grips so many of us? What value do academic researchers from the social sciences and humanities bring to our daily conversations and debates?

As scholars, we are obligated to challenge deceptions and distortions. We are obligated to defend knowledge, facts, and reason. We are compelled to stand up for science, for humanistic values, and for the institutions that we've built to support them. All are under attack.

Trump may well be an idiosyncratic and extreme figure, but he reached the highest office in the land by riding deep and powerful currents of American political culture. The sources of his authority and of his enduring popular support come from his frequent appeals to race, to religion, and to free-market capitalism. They are strengthened by his role as a celebrity provocateur in a national media system that, by comparative standards, is organized around competition for advertising revenue and audience size above all else.

This book places Trump's ascendance in the context of these formidable structural forces. Taken together, the essays gathered here identify and explain the conditions that allow someone like Trump to be taken seriously and even to win a national election. They help make sense of the current moment but also anticipate future situations. Though Trump will not be president forever, the issues his victory raises will not go away when he leaves office. We want this book to be a toolkit whose utility outlasts any one person's political career.

The sources of authority that the contributors to this book draw upon are quite different from those that helped legitimate Donald

Trump to his supporters. Some of those who come from the social sciences appeal to knowledge that was introduced, tested, and verified in universities and make claims that, like all scientific findings, will be subjected to ongoing examination until the next advance. Those trained in the humanities and interpretive social sciences root their observations in meticulous parsing of the historical record and methodical examination of social worlds. They value precise, careful language, in contrast to Trump's word salads. Their conclusions are subject to shared lineages of logic, reason, and ethics.

The humanists and interpretive social scientists whose work is featured here have been strong champions of the values that Trump seeks to overthrow when he says he wants to "make America great again": feminism, anti-imperialism, multiculturalism, anti-homophobia, environmentalism, and a commitment to amplifying voices that have been muffled for most of this country's history. They've advanced an egalitarian agenda that is antithetical to those of Trump and his staunchest supporters.

Whether scientific or humanistic, the scholarly traditions that lie at the root of this book threaten Trump's authority. It's not surprising, then, that Trump has threatened to curtail support for science, social science, and the humanities and to all higher education institutions that support them. As Trump sees it, he alone decides what truth will be and how it will guide power. We reject this vision, and in the pages that follow we offer an alternative approach.

The authors here come from different academic fields and bring diverse perspectives. They cover a wide range of topics: race relations, civil rights and liberties, international law, religion, protest and dissent, crime, inequality, immigration, sexuality and gender, climate change, capitalism, education, science policy, diplomacy, nuclear conflict, national security, gun control and violence, class and culture, reproductive rights, health care, and the media, among others.

Our hope is that each contribution sparks deeply informed, carefully reasoned debate about what President Trump and the radical political project he is advancing mean for America's democratic experiment. Together, we want to examine the threat of antidemocracy in America because everything is at stake. ▮

PART I

The Crisis

Where We Are

RESOURCE EXTRACTION

MICHELLE WILDE ANDERSON

T rump has a range of cons going, but one of the most outrageous is this: he is about to fleece his working-class supporters in the Rust Belt, coal country, and the rural Pacific Northwest. When he does, we will all suffer the losses.

These are the most land-rich, cash-poor regions of our country. They are places where many people feel that their birthright is in the soil itself: the coal seams, old-growth forests, shale gas, and even gold ore. Such resources may be scarce in the world, but they look plentiful if you live in their midst. It is easy to understand the enraged sense of stolen prosperity that follows—a suspicion that distant cities teeming with people in suits have locked local families away from their patrimony. What if you were very poor but looked around and thought your surroundings could have made you very rich?

Trump has told these communities that he will turn regional land into cash. What he will not tell them is that *the cash would not be for them*. Today's dramatic inequality and the ownership structure of our extractive industries mean that a small number of multinational corporations are poised to confiscate America's patrimony of forests and fuels, paying for the right to do so with just a few crumbs for a few years. Families in these areas will lose, and because burning fossil fuels and clear-cutting mature forests accelerate climate change, everyone else will lose with them.

Along with his EPA Administrator Scott Pruitt, Trump is pursuing structural reforms that reflect the principle that getting regulation out of the way of resource extraction will build our wealth as a nation. Their claim reminds me of an early American legal doctrine called the "rule of capture," which governed mobile natural resources like oil, gas, foxes, and fish. When it came to wild things, you were free to take whatever you could, as fast as you could. That's what made it yours. If you could afford the biggest ocean nets or oil wells, more power (property) to you. Leaving resources fallow was prosperity squandered. This was before most environmental science or the labor movement, so it didn't matter if you left water in a nearby stream undrinkable, paid your workers too little to live on, or risked their safety on the job. It didn't matter if you depleted the supply in ways that hurt future generations.

Many of us who teach this rule in law school play a scene from the film *There Will Be Blood* to explain how it worked, and the scene is a useful metaphor here as well. The character Daniel Plainview, an early 1900s oil baron, is thundering at a whimpering man named Eli Sunday. Sunday has come to offer Plainview a lease to draw oil from under Sunday's property, but he's too late. Plainview's leases to surrounding wells had already allowed him to empty Sunday's oil deposit. "That land has been had," Plainview says, "Nothing you can do about it." Staggering drunk in his private bowling alley, Plainview spits violently as he explains: "Drainage! Drainage. Eli . . . you boy. Drained dry. I'm so sorry. Here, if you have a milkshake, and I have a milkshake, and I have a straw. . . . Now, my straw reaches acrooooooooooss the room and starts to drink your milkshake. I drink your milkshake! I drink it up!"

Trump wants a government that only works for the likes of Daniel Plainview—not for Plainview's employees, neighbors, or smaller competitors and certainly not for the public. The key to selling this agenda is the illusion that anyone can be Plainview. This is the president who brought us books like *Trump: How to Get Rich* (yes, his name is in the title) and *Why We Want You to Be Rich*. A Twitter message from an account in "the Mountains, West Virginia" schooled me on how much people want to believe this. "Don't fall for the Marxist propaganda," it said. "The movement should be to make poor people wealthy."

The heist, though, is that we are all still Eli Sunday, and the big mouth about to drain our milkshake is no longer a regional, individual powerhouse like Plainview. Returning to a winner-take-all system for natural resources in 2017 benefits a small group of global industrial giants and their few owners. Take Peabody Energy, for instance, the world's largest coal company, whose 2016 bankruptcy filing allowed it to restructure its obligations to bondholders, pensioners, and government agencies. That bankruptcy reaped a $15 million stock bonus for its chief executive, and hundreds of millions of dollars for six hedge funds that are all based in New York City or Connecticut. Or consider some of the big timber stands and mills in Northern California, which were drawn together in 1891 by lumber titan C. R. Johnson and his family company, Union Lumber. In 1969, Union Lumber was sold to the Boise Cascade Corporation, which was sold to Georgia-Pacific in 1973, one of the largest paper-products companies in the world. In 2005, the Koch Industries—one of the biggest companies of any kind in the country—rolled the Georgia-Pacific conglomerate into their even bigger empire.

With their power and $3.1 million to lobby lawmakers early this year, the Koch brothers helped write a wave of deregulation measures and confirm Scott Pruitt, who is poised to deliver our land wealth to them for a song. Pruitt is using every tool he can find to transform the EPA into a concierge service for the largest oil and gas, chemical-manufacturing, and coal companies. He is likely courting them as donors for his own political future.

Applying the rule of capture to today's world means crossing the wires of big capital with rural poverty, amid powerful extractive technologies that minimize job creation. There is money to be made for sure, but it will flow to the biggest corporations and their C-Suites. Beyond them is just a bit of trickle down here and there. As in other industries, wages for jobs in the coal industry are not keeping pace with the economy, even as executive pay soars. Unionized miners still make a good living, but only 2.5 percent of coal miners were covered by a union as of 2016. This leaves most coal miners competing for short-term jobs that lack health benefits and pull in less than twenty dollars per hour while they last.

Meanwhile, Trump's proposed 2018 budget eliminates funding for the Appalachian Regional Commission (ARC) and the U.S. Economic Development Administration, which have long supported downsized coal miners and new businesses in Appalachia. While Congress acted in May to find taxpayer funding to cover health benefits for 22,000 retired coal miners whose employers had gone bankrupt, there is as yet no fix to address those miners' unfunded pensions. So far, Trump's ideas for rebuilding infrastructure would only work for projects that can pay down debt with high usage fees over time (like bridge tolls, airport taxes, and rising water rates). This will mean little to no infrastructure work on the urgent projects needed in older areas where residents cannot afford to pay more for what they need.

Pruitt holds up his home state of Oklahoma as a promise: look how a state rich in fossil fuels becomes rich in money. But it really should be a warning. For more than twenty-five years, incomes for poor and middle-class families in Oklahoma have fallen or stagnated, despite dramatic growth among the state's wealthiest households. Posing in a hardhat, as Pruitt so often does these days, does not a working man make.

This would all be hard enough to fix if a rule of capture for America only mattered in terms of monopolistic power and rising income inequality. Even that would require a better model for sharing the prosperity of our land: whether through tax and labor reforms or regional royalty systems like the one in Alaska, where oil and gas extraction yields checks for every single resident.

Unfortunately, it is even more than wealth and poverty at stake. When it comes to natural resources, our wealth is subject to contamination, waste, and depletion. It matters *how* things are done— whether a shale-gas well or a coal mine is operated so as to protect area water supplies, whether the land left behind is safe and usable for other purposes. It matters if we choose methods of harvesting fish and timber that permit regeneration, especially because sustainable practices maintain more jobs.

The finitude of finite resources means that at some point fossil fuels are gone for good, even as the greenhouse gases they leave are here to stay. Even trees are stubbornly slow to regrow, such that clearing the remaining stands of federal old-growth forests in the Pacific Northwest would only offer a short burst of logging before starting a seventy-five-year waiting game on lower value farm trees.

And, of course, in the age of climate change, our stewardship of fossil fuels and forests has global implications. Hurricanes Harvey, Irma, and Maria provide a reminder that the raging storms and rising seas of climate change will be cruel to rich and poor alike, but those who are most economically vulnerable may be least able to rebuild. The recent years of catastrophic wildfires and droughts in the West make clear that it is in our vital personal interest not to let the fossil-fuel industry grow at the expense of us all.

I think the road out of here is to return the way we came. Here is what I mean: For decades, people in our land-rich, cash-poor regions have looked for answers to the puzzle of natural wealth and pervasive poverty in their communities. Too few of our environmental regulations or other policies included large-scale government efforts (in education, economic development, and land reclamation) to ensure a just transition beyond an economy based on logging and mining. America has yet to see a major national investment in rural education to answer the hardships of the machine age in mills and mines, which has cost these regions so many jobs. Other than some protesters in Seattle, few tried to make a social movement fighting for fairness in the global markets for building materials like steel and lumber that were driving down the value of our domestic supplies.

In the absence of alternative ways to make a living, in the absence of honesty about the ways that automation and globalization were replacing and offshoring jobs, people looked for answers. Major industries provided them: environmental regulation alone was to blame. This has always been the winning move for extractive industries and consolidated agriculture.

We've seen this in California for ages. Most recently, during our devastating drought amplified by climate change, the agribusiness giants of the Westlands Water District funded a $1.1 million "astroturf" campaign to convey that what was good for Westlands was good for California's impoverished, drought-stricken farmworkers. (Now that Trump has installed a Westlands lobbyist as the deputy secretary of the Department of the Interior, they may not need such campaigns.) But the truth is that the Westlands businesses keep down those same farmworkers' wage and labor protections, and their thirsty cash crops undermine the water supply for farmworker homes. The political reality is that when a paycheck from agribusiness is all you've got (even if it's less than subsistence wages), and no one else in the state seems to acknowledge you exist, you begin to believe the boss's needs are your needs.

Just as environmental groups can't show up at the eleventh hour of a terrible drought causing job losses and say they care about farmworkers, so too the American Left can't keep ignoring our land-rich, cash-poor regions. No one can afford for Trump and Pruitt to be the only people who show up holding a plan. "Drill, baby, drill" starts looking pretty good if there is no other prospect of making rent—even if Exxon wrote the plan and everyone knows that drilling, baby, requires more machines than men.

To show up with a plan, I think, means this: blue voters and politicians in the cities, state governments, and federal delegations of purple, resource-rich states like West Virginia, Pennsylvania, Michigan, and Colorado have to seize the political moment to issue a vocal, organized demand for three things: (1) ambitious, transformative investments (including for tuition relief) in community colleges and universities in declining urban and rural areas; (2) capital investments in small businesses as a foundation for economic development; and (3) a jobs program (expanded from the American Recovery and Reinvestment Act model) that meets urgent needs in these regions, such as rebuilding decaying water and wastewater infrastructure, thinning the overstocked western forests that threaten rural counties with wildfires, decontaminating waterways and land sullied by fossil-fuel extraction, and treating the opioid-addiction crisis.

This demand is for Trump as well as all the Democrats in Congress—that is, the two groups whose immediate political future most depends on a serious campaign for the stabilization and reinvention of declining regions. If big business is the only hope in town, it will always divide households' urgent, short-term economic interests from collective environmental safety interests.

Sooner or later, the Left is going to have to adopt a platform that ties environmental justice and economic justice together in a single movement. *That platform must be rooted in reinvestment, not just regulation.*

I am very sympathetic to the argument that our land rich, cash-poor areas have had their patrimony locked down. But they are no better off if instead, after a few years of a few low-wage jobs, it has been consumed by the industrial behemoths of the Second Gilded Age. A future climate that is safe for all of us is my patrimony, too, and I will stand with the Rust Belt, coal country, and our timberlands to make sure that their poverty doesn't drive them to sell the riches of their land for just the hourly wages they need. That means guarding our shared interests and providing ambitious alternatives so that the Daniel Plainviews of our times can never say to us, as Plainview said to Eli Sunday, "You're just the afterbirth."

CONFRONTING MANHOOD AFTER TRUMP

LISA WADE

I f it were fiction, it would have been dismissed as preposterous. America elected a grotesque, slobbering id to the highest office of the most powerful country in the world: a thundering narcissist who, without irony, describes himself as "the world's greatest person."[1] And central to his persona is a vulgar and vindictive masculinity, not cold and calculating, as is his vice president's, but hot and festering, like an open wound.

Presidential campaigns are always referendums on what "good" and "real" men are like, but Trump's unabashed sexism and incapacity for mortification is like nothing anyone alive has seen before.[2] On the campaign trail, he threw emasculating barbs at supposedly lesser men, spewed sexist insults at uppity women, sexually objectified underage girls, and coveted the totalitarian power of dictators.[3] He bragged about pussies and penis size and how he'd never rape an ugly woman. Instead of cratering, his campaign soared.

There's a substantial proportion of men—and women, too—who are willing to tolerate this vile enactment of masculinity, mixed (as it usually is) with racism, homophobia, religious hatred, and nationalism. There are also those who have long been waiting, yearning, *lusting* for someone like him. To those on Breitbart,

4Chan, and /r/The_Donald; to those high on toxic right-wing radio; to those hiding in plain sight throughout our society, Trump emerged from the Republican presidential primary not just a candidate but a champion: a hero to those mostly white men who bristle at the idea of sharing America's prosperity with those whom they see as inferior.[4] Trump was perhaps not wrong to believe that he could "stand in the middle of Fifth Avenue and shoot somebody" and not lose voters, so long as that somebody was female, black or brown, Muslim, or a migrant.[5]

As president, Trump has assembled the most male-dominated staff in decades and appointed known white nationalists to senior positions. With the help of a group of (mostly) men in Congress, he is attacking antidiscrimination and equal-pay laws; health, contraceptive, and prenatal care; foreign aid for women's advancement; national guidelines to address sexual assault on college campuses; and any chance that the highest court will act to protect civil rights. Thanks to the craven complicity of the Republican Party, Trump is undermining participatory, broad-based democracy before our very eyes. Indeed, there is nothing about his constitution—barring, perhaps, his laziness—that suggests that he will voluntarily cede power when his term (or terms) are up.

This is a historical schism, a realignment of reality that requires a rethinking of who we are, what we do, and why.[6] Accordingly, Trump's rise demands that feminists and their allies learn to think and fight differently. And we must learn fast.

The first thing that must go is the belief among progressives that we are on some fateful journey to a better place.[7] We know that America's grand democratic vision of "all men are created equal" didn't initially include all men or any women and that we have never granted the promised equality. Yet many of us still hold fast to the idea that America is a great nation, managing the cognitive dissonance by envisioning the country as on a journey *toward* perfection. As Martin Luther King Jr. famously said, echoing the abolitionist Theodore Parker, "The arc of the moral universe is long, but it bends toward justice."

Among feminists, the reigning metaphor reflecting this optimism is the "stalled revolution," a phrase introduced by the sociologist Arlie Hochschild in 1989.[8] Her intent was to draw attention to both the progress that had been made (women's enthusiastic embrace of the traits and activities previously restricted to men) and the progress yet to be made (men's embrace of those previously restricted to women). Implicit in the metaphor is the idea that we will have reached gender equality when men and women alike embrace both halves of their humanity: masculinity *and* femininity. As a nation, Hochschild argued, we are halfway there. To fully revolutionize gender relations, we just need to get moving again.

Thirty years is a long life for a metaphor, and it's still here because it's been useful and descriptive, reflecting a lived reality. But we are in Trump's America now. The metaphor of the stalled revolution, however useful it has been, posits a linear past and future. It assumes that stall is equivalent to stasis: that we are still in the driver's seat, the path is still there, and we're still aiming at something good. The metaphor doesn't allow for the possibility that the world has shifted around us, setting us on a path that we may no longer want to be on. It certainly doesn't contain the prospect that we are—that we *have* been—moving toward something terrible.

In fact, Trump's masculinity is what we call a toxic masculinity. In the pre-Trump era, the modifier was used to differentiate bad masculine ideals from good ones. Toxic masculinities, some claimed, were behind sexual assault, mass shootings, and the weird thing where men refuse to wear sunscreen, but they didn't reflect masculinity *generally*, so one had to leave that idea alone. But we can only give masculinity so many modifiers for so long before we have to confront the possibility that it is masculinity itself that has become the problem.

Feminist critiques of projects like Sheryl Sandberg's *Lean In* (2013), for example—those that exhort women to compete with men in male-dominated workplaces—suggest that women's embrace of masculinity may be good for individual women but actually quite bad for society.[9] Relishing competition over cooperation, taking pleasure in beating opponents, and showing no remorse for hoarding wealth and exploiting power are features of a masculine "politics of domination."[10] Is it really a better world if half of the winners of this game are women?

Meanwhile, sociologists have argued that men are perfectly capable of mixing femininity into their gender performances in ways that uphold men's dominance.[11] Anti-rape campaigns like "My Strength Is Not for Hurting" and pro-family ones like the Promise Keepers, for example, both involve men invoking a feminine ethic of care that, nonetheless, positions their control of women and other men as good and right.[12] This is a benevolent sexism instead of a hostile one, but it is sexism nonetheless.[13]

As the sociologist Raewyn Connell once observed, men becoming more feminine and women becoming more masculine *may* produce gender equality, but it "may do just the reverse."[14] Indeed, such an outcome likely wouldn't even be good for most men. An ideology that equates masculinity with "winning" is one in which only a handful of men come out on top.[15] Poor and working-class men, old men, queer men, trans men, men of color, immigrant men, and men with disabilities disproportionately lose. So do men who find no pleasure in domination. Ironically, this is often why men who *are* failing in this macho competition—the economically struggling, the unmanly nerds, and even sometimes gay men—are among the most obviously sexist. They may be at the bottom of a hierarchy of men, they reason, but at least they're not women.

Applying these ideas to Trump's presidency, it's hard to argue that the high-profile, high-status, and highly paid positions of Kellyanne Conway and Sarah Huckabee Sanders, not to mention the presence in the White House of his daughter, Ivanka, are doing anything to undermine gender inequality in the United States. Quite the opposite. Meanwhile, Trump's claim to be the sole person capable of saving America—captured in his appalling comment about the Middle East: "I alone can fix it"— positions him as an omnipotent patriarch.[16] He says he is protecting Americans when he bans Muslims from the United States, calls for a wall on the Mexican border, and threatens nuclear war with North Korea, often specifically invoking women's sexual vulnerability when he does so.[17] If Trump has his way, most men will suffer, too. His policies—from his tax breaks to the deregulation of industry—hurt everyone except those at the very top.

Is this where the stalled revolution is now headed?

The quaint balance of masculinity and femininity that the metaphor promised is no longer desirable, if it ever was. Instead of advocating that women compete with men on masculine terms and men mix in just enough femininity to distance themselves from the most toxic versions of masculinity, we need to start being honest about what being a man has come to mean. Trump's rise has made it terrifyingly clear that his toxic version is not at all peripheral to twenty-first-century modern masculinity. It is central. It is authoritarian. And it is lethal.

If we're going to survive both President Trump and the kind of people he has emboldened, we need to attack masculinity directly. I don't mean that we should recuperate masculinity—that is, press men to identify with a kinder, gentler version of it—I mean that we should reject the idea that men have a psychic need to distinguish themselves from women in order to feel good about themselves. This idea is sexist on its face and it's unsettling that we so rarely think of it that way.

In fact, we should be as suspicious of males who strongly identify as men as we are of white people who strongly identify as white. We should understand, in hindsight, that one of the reasons women were so keen to embrace masculinity in the first place was because it feels good to feel superior. And we should recognize, as well, that it is men's belief that they *should* be superior to women and other men that is the cause of so much of their rage, self-hatred, and suffering.

We are here in Trump's America in part because we have been too delicate in our treatment of dangerous ideas. The problem is not toxic masculinity; it's that masculinity is toxic. Its appeal is its alluring promise that if we obey it, we can all bask in a sense of superiority over *someone*. It's simply not compatible with liberty and justice for all.

If we are going to finish the gender revolution, then, we need to call masculinity out as a hazardous ideology and denounce anyone who chooses to identify with it. We need to stop talking about what it means to be a "real man" or an "empowered woman" and begin talking, instead, about what it means to be a good person and a good citizen. Our nation's future depends upon it.

NOTES

Revised May 24, 2018.

1. Greg Miller, Julie Vitkovsaya, and Reuben Fischer-Baum, "'This Deal Will Make Me Look Terrible': Full Transcripts of Trump's Calls with Mexico and Australia," *Washington Post*, August 3, 2017, https://www.washingtonpost.com/graphics/2017/politics/australia-mexico-transcripts.
2. Jackson Katz, *Man Enough? Donald Trump, Hillary Clinton, and the Politics of Presidential Masculinity* (Northampton, MA: Interlink, 2016).

3. Kristen Barber, "Satire as Protest in the Women's March," *Gender and Society*, April 12, 2017, https://gendersociety.wordpress.com/2017/04/12/satire-as-protest-in-the-womens-march/; James W. Messerschmidt and Tristan Bridges, "Trump and the Politics of Fluid Masculinities," *Gender and Society*, July 21, 2017, https://gendersociety.wordpress.com/2017/07/21/trump-and-the-politics-of-fluid-masculinities/; C. J. Pascoe, "Who Is a Real Man? The Gender of Trumpism," *Masculinities and Social Change* 6, no. 2 (2017), http://hipatiapress.com/hpjournals/index.php/mcs/article/view/2745/pdf.

4. Michael Kimmel, *Angry White Men: American Masculinity at the End of an Era* (New York: Nation Books, 2015).

5. Jeremy Diamond, "Trump: I Could 'Shoot Somebody and I Wouldn't Lose Voters,'" CNN, January 24, 2016, http://www.cnn.com/2016/01/23/politics/donald-trump-shoot-somebody-support/index.html.

6. Ann Swidler, "Culture in Action: Symbols and Strategies," *American Sociological Review* 51, no. 2 (1986), https://www.jstor.org/stable/2095521.

7. For a discussion of the role of optimism in discourses of modernity, see Anthony Giddens, *The Consequences of Modernity* (Stanford, CA: Stanford University Press, 1990).

8. Arlie Russell Hochschild, with Anne Machung, *The Second Shift: Working Parents and the Revolution at Home* (New York: Viking Penguin, 1989).

9. Linda Burnham, "Lean In and One Percent Feminism," *Portside*, March 26, 2013, http://portside.org/2013-03-26/lean-and-one-percent-feminism.

10. bell hooks, *Talking Back: Thinking Feminist, Thinking Black* (Boston: South End Press, 1989).

11. Tristan Bridges and C. J. Pascoe, "Hybrid Masculinities: New Directions in the Sociology of Men and Masculinities," *Sociology Compass* 3, no. 3 (2014), http://onlinelibrary.wiley.com/doi/10.1111/soc4.12134/abstract.

12. Melanie Heath, "Soft-Boiled Masculinity: Renegotiating Gender and Racial Ideologies in the Promise Keepers Movement," *Gender and Society* 17, no. 3 (2003), http://journals.sagepub.com/doi/abs/10.1177/0891243203017003008; N. Tatiana Masters, "'My Strength Is Not for Hurting': Men's Anti-Rape Websites and Their Construction of Masculinity and Male Sexuality," *Sexualities* 13, no. 1 (2010), http://journals.sagepub.com/doi/abs/10.1177/1363460709346115?journalCode=sexa; Michael Murphy, "Can 'Men' Stop Rape? Visualizing Gender in the 'My Strength Is Not for Hurting' Rape Prevention Campaign," *Men and Masculinities* 12, no. 1 (2009), http://journals.sagepub.com/doi/abs/10.1177/1097184X09331752.

13. Peter Glick and Susan Fiske, "Hostile and Benevolent Sexism: Measuring Ambivalent Sexist Attitudes Toward Women," *Psychology of Women Quarterly* 21, no. 1 (1997), http://journals.sagepub.com/doi/abs/10.1111/j.1471-6402.1997.tb00104.x.

14. R. W. Connell, *Gender and Power: Society, the Person, and Sexual Politics* (Cambridge: Polity, 1987), 283.

15. Kimberle Crenshaw, "Mapping the Margins: Intersectionality, Identity Politics, and Violence Against Women of Color," *Stanford Law Review* 43, no. 6 (1991), https://www.jstor.org/stable/1229039.

16. James W. Messerschmidt and Tristan Bridges, "Trump and the Politics of Fluid Masculinities," *Gender and Society,* July 21, 2017, https://gendersociety.wordpress.com/2017/07/21/trump-and-the-politics-of-fluid-masculinities/.

17. Amanda Taub, "Portraying Muslims as a Threat to Women, Donald Trump Echoes 'Us vs. Them' Refrain," *New York Times,* August 16, 2016, https://www.nytimes.com/2016/08/17/us/politics/donald-trump-muslims-immigration.htmlo; Washington Post Staff, "Full Text: Donald Trump Announces a Presidential Bid," *Washington Post,* June 16, 2015, https://www.washingtonpost.com/news/post-politics/wp/2015/06/16/full-text-donald-trump-announces-a-presidential-bid/.

PREDATORY REAL ESTATE

THOMAS J. SUGRUE

O n a clear day, from his sixty-eighth-floor penthouse on Fifth Avenue, President Trump can survey America's greatest metropolis. To the west is a glass-and-steel forest of luxury towers bordering Central Park and Columbus Circle, where international magnates park their capital in extravagant luxury condominiums. To the east are celebrity-architect-designed high rises that have recently sprung up along the East River, turning former industrial wastelands into some of the world's priciest real estate. Off in the distance are the vast low-rise landscapes of the outer boroughs and suburbs, extending to the horizon.

Trump's New York displays all of the contradictions of twenty-first-century metropolitan America. It is starkly divided by income and wealth, an embodiment of the inequalities that define and distort American politics today. Decades after the civil rights revolution of the 1950s and 1960s, metro New York ranks near the top of the most racially divided metropolitan areas in the United States. New York's public schools, the most segregated in the nation, defy *Brown v. Board of Education*. The gaps in funding and student achievement are enormous.

New York's housing is also increasingly unaffordable. Much of Manhattan and Brooklyn is out of reach to all but the wealthiest.

Well-paid financial executives, marketers, and web developers have colonized formerly working-class neighborhoods such as Williamsburg and Bushwick. Further afield, Crown Heights and Prospect Heights, once enclaves of Caribbean immigrants, are rapidly gentrifying and whitening. If current patterns hold, much of Harlem below 125th Street (or SoHa, as some real estate brokers are attempting to rebrand it) will soon be majority white.

Donald Trump may have vaulted to the White House with the backing of small-town and rural voters, but he is one of the few big-city-born and raised occupants of the White House in the last century. He has spent nearly all of his seven decades living in New York City. His fate and that of the metropolis are fundamentally linked. Trump rose to power through plunder and predation, aided and abetted by public policies that allowed him to build a fortune in real estate development. He is a beneficiary—personally and politically—of the staggering class and race inequalities that define modern American life.

A native of Queens, Donald Trump was the son and heir to Fred Trump, a scrappy and ruthless developer of housing for New York's white working and middle class. An outer-borough nativist and one-time Klan supporter, the senior Trump profited mightily from the federal government's massive intervention in the real-estate industry, which began in the Great Depression. His fortune was premised on strict racial segregation, a process whose legacies still shape the geography of urban and suburban America.

Fred Trump's most famous tenant, Woody Guthrie, lambasted his landlord:

I suppose
Old Man Trump knows
Just how much
Racial Hate

he stirred up
In the bloodpot of human hearts
When he drawed
That color line
Here at his
Eighteen hundred family project.

Donald Trump followed his father's discriminatory path. In 1973, shortly after he took the helm of his father's firm, the U.S. Department of Justice filed a lawsuit accusing the Trump Organization of persistent discrimination by race in its housing developments. One of Trump's doormen told investigators that "if a black person came to 2650 Ocean Parkway and inquired about an apartment for rent . . . I should tell him that the rent was twice as much as it really was, in order that he could not afford the apartment."

The future president fought the charges and filed a $100 million countersuit accusing the federal government of defamation, a pattern that would play out again and again over his long career. The Trump Organization refused to admit culpability but eventually settled the civil-rights case, agreeing to make apartments available on a nondiscriminatory basis. But that was a sham. In 1978, the Department of Justice charged that Trump continued to discriminate against African Americans.

The Trump family built its fortune on discriminatory practices that devastated urban America. The sociologists Douglas Massey and Nancy Denton coined the term "American apartheid" to describe the deep racial rifts that divided New York and most major metropolitan areas in the United States (especially in the Northeast and Midwest) into racialized territories. The housing segregation that made the Trump family's fortune deprived generations of African Americans of decent housing, access to growing job markets, and well-funded schools. Fred Trump may have been a Klan supporter, but by the time Donald was running the firm, discrimination happened behind closed doors—in banks, real-estate firms, and rental offices. The invisibility of this new version of Jim Crow made racial separation seem inevitable, the result of the natural workings of the market or, as ordinary Americans put it, "Birds of a feather flock together."

Endemic housing segregation fueled an urban crisis characterized by a deeply polarized politics of race, and it contributed mightily to massive urban disinvestment and depopulation as whites fled to homogenous suburbs. The Trumps, however, always found ways to profit from crisis. In the late 1970s, big cities, desperate to attract new investment, began to provide incentives to large-scale real estate developers. The Trump Organization was at the front of the queue for taking advantage of tax abatements, zoning variances, and other giveaways, all designed to "bring the city back" by building tourist destinations and upscale housing in downtowns.

In 1979, as New York was slowly climbing out of its fiscal collapse—and as the city's air was still darkened by the soot from burning buildings in the South Bronx—the gaudy Trump Tower began to rise on Fifth Avenue, distinguished by its vast atrium, which was ostentatiously adorned with brass handrails (polished twice a month) and rare Breccia Pernice marble cladding imported from Italy. The building benefited from a New York City tax-abatement program (which the Trump Organization sued the Koch administration to get). Over the next three decades, the Trumps took in at least $885 million in tax breaks to develop luxury apartments, hotels, and other properties throughout Manhattan. New York's Grand Hyatt, one of Donald Trump's earliest successes, alone cost New York City more than $360 million in abated taxes.

Beginning in the Reagan era, Trump also took advantage of the deregulation of credit markets to fund his ventures. He expanded his empire outside of New York, availing his firm of state programs to reinvigorate declining cities, most famously New Jersey's desperate effort to reinvent decrepit Atlantic City as the Las Vegas of the East. In the early 1990s, he built a (fragile) fortune in casino gambling, pocketing the nickels and quarters of desperate working-class and lower-middle-class bettors who, left behind in a stagnant economy, clung to the dream of hitting the jackpot on rigged slot machines.

New Jersey bet big and lost bigger on gambling as a tool for urban revitalization, but even as Trump's casino foundered and nearly brought his empire down, he leveraged his name into a next generation of profits that included a diverse portfolio of overseas branding schemes, entertainment ventures, and vanity golf courses. Trump has also continued to profit from his urban real-estate investments, most recently the new, heavily subsidized Trump International Hotel in Washington, DC, just a few blocks from the White House.

Predatory real estate is the power center of Trumpism. The president's former campaign chair, Paul Manafort, made a small fortune in housing development before heading overseas to lobby for dictators. In the late 1980s, Manafort supped at the trough of Ronald Reagan's troubled Department of Housing and Urban Development, receiving nearly $43 million in federal subsidies to construct shabby affordable housing in suburban New Jersey.

Trump is also surrounded by aides who made their fortunes, in whole or in part, through fraudulent and predatory lending practices. Investigators reported that Secretary of the Treasury Steven Mnuchin's OneWest bank foreclosed on tens of thousands of homeowners and engaged in deceptive practices, from shredding borrowers' applications for loan modification to backdating mortgages. Commerce Secretary Wilbur Ross bought American Home Mortgage Servicing, one of the country's largest predatory lenders.

The new administration has prioritized easing banking and lending regulations, including eviscerating the Consumer Financial Protection Board, which protects borrowers from deceptive lending practices.

The aftermath of the 2008 housing crisis provided yet more opportunities for profit and plunder at the expense of low-income Americans, especially racial minorities, desperate for good housing. The president's aide-de-camp and son-in-law Jared Kushner led the ranks of real estate investors who swept into communities ravaged by foreclosures, gobbling up apartments and modest homes at bargain prices. After minimal repairs and cosmetic renovations, they reap substantial profits by charging high rents, issuing exorbitant penalties for late payments or technical violations of lease terms, and slapping tenants with lawsuits and steep legal fees if they cannot pay up. Between 2011 and 2014, Kushner's firm acquired nearly 20,000 units in multifamily buildings, mostly "distress-ridden, Class B" apartment complexes in declining suburbs in Ohio, New Jersey, and Maryland, with some 5,000 in metro Baltimore alone.

Trump presides over a deeply unequal metropolitan landscape that has provided him, his advisers, and other bankers and real-estate developers untold wealth in the last forty years. Those practices have also played a key role in widening the gaps between rich and poor across American metropolitan areas. Since the 1970s, as the sociologists Sean Reardon and Kendra Bischoff have shown, American metros have grown sharply more segregated by class. America's "haves"—wealthy, mostly white, highly educated professionals—have clustered in elite suburbs but also in upscale urban neighborhoods. By contrast, working-class people are trapped in central cities and secondhand suburbs, places with out-of-fashion housing, shrinking commercial districts, collapsing tax bases, underfunded schools, and decaying infrastructure.

Inequality manifests itself starkly in housing markets. The Great Recession swept up millions of Americans, overwhelmingly lower-middle-class and working-class, in a wave of foreclosures. People of color—especially African Americans and Latinos, including many who were migrating to suburbs—were disproportionately victimized by predatory lending, which wiped out their precarious household wealth. In 2015, just as Trump launched his campaign for the presidency, African American and Latino households had only about one-twentieth the household wealth of whites, largely because of the subprime crisis and the collapse of the real estate market.

Just as devastating has been the collapse of the affordable rental market. Between 2010 and 2016, the stock of affordable housing units in the United States dropped by 60 percent. The *Washington Post* reported that "affordable housing without a government subsidy is becoming extinct." Left to fend for themselves, a growing number of low-income Americans are victims of profiteering landlords.

Princeton's Matthew Desmond has written powerfully about the crisis in affordable housing in major metropolitan areas. Working-class and poor people, unable to afford mortgages and lacking options in increasingly expensive cities, are trapped in units that are usually overpriced, poorly located, and badly maintained. One of the most common sights on sidewalks in poor neighborhoods are piles of shabby furniture, toys, and clothes, the telltale signs that poor families have been evicted for missing a rent payment.

Trump's urban vision accounts for none of these realities. On the campaign trail, he offered a *Bonfire of the Vanities* view of American cities. On one hand, he trumpeted his development acumen, his ability to spin dollars out of New York's high-rise air. On the other hand, he painted a cartoonish picture of the urban apocalypse. "Our inner cities are a disaster," Trump declared during his final debate against Hillary Clinton. "You get shot walking to the store. They have no education. They have no jobs." Trump dusted off venerable "blame the victim" rhetoric, pointing his finger at gang members, new immigrants, and poor people themselves.

Again and again, the real-estate tycoon invoked the "inner cities," 1960s shorthand for impoverished nonwhite neighborhoods skirting decaying downtowns. And he turned blame away from failed reinvestment strategies, tax breaks, and predatory lending practices, instead lambasting his political enemies. "The Democrats have failed completely in the inner cities," he told an audience in Akron, Ohio. "For those hurting the most, who have been failed and failed by their politicians, year after year, failure after failure, worse numbers after worse numbers, poverty, rejection, horrible education, no houses, no homes, no ownership, crime at levels that nobody has seen. You could go to war zones in countries that we're fighting and it's safer than living in some of our inner cities that are run by the Democrats."

Trump's use of the term "inner city" and his reflexive association of "urban" and "minority" do not capture the changed reality of metropolitan America. Today, more than half of African Americans live in suburbs, as do a majority of immigrants. Many of them are refugees from urban neighborhoods marred by run-down housing, decaying infrastructure, underfunded schools, and overpriced, often shabby rental units. In fact, poverty rates are growing the most rapidly in suburbs and rural areas, *not* in urban America.

As president, Trump has inherited an urban-policy mess that his administration will almost certainly make worse. American urban policy has been hobbled since the 1970s, when federal and state urban spending plummeted and white backlash and austerity measures combined with devastating effect. The Nixon and Carter administrations trimmed urban spending, channeling money to city agencies through underfunded programs such as the Community Development Block Grant program. In Reagan's eight years in office, federal urban expenditures fell from 12 percent to a mere 3 percent of domestic spending. Reagan also gutted the Department of Housing and Urban Development, which struggled with huge budget cuts and incompetent leadership. In the meantime, many state governments, often dominated by suburban and rural legislators and struggling with federal cutbacks themselves, also dramatically axed their budgets. In a polity that had become majority suburban in the 1980s, cities had fewer and fewer friends in high places.

In the 1990s and 2000s, neither Democrats nor Republicans spent much political capital on cities. Federal funds went to trendy but largely ineffective "enterprise" and "empowerment" zones, which offered tax abatements for commercial development in ravaged neighborhoods. Federal dollars went to the destruction of public housing. Its replacement with mixed-market and subsidized developments was in theory a good idea; in practice, however, these were built on too small a scale to have any real effect other than lengthening waiting lists for what little publicly funded affordable housing remained.

The Obama administration created a new office of urban affairs, but instead of reinvesting in quality public housing and other vital urban infrastructure, it put its efforts into small-scale public-private partnerships, revamping "empowerment zones" into "Promise Neighborhoods." Other proposed Obama-era initiatives that would have benefited cities, including substantial funding for mass transit and decaying infrastructure, could not muster support in the GOP-controlled Congress.

Meanwhile, the wreckage caused by the Great Recession has spread poverty and insecurity not just throughout urban America but deep into previously aspirational suburbs too. What is needed, in response, is not just a reinvigorated federal urban policy but, more generally, a metropolitan-revitalization program capable of tackling the economic woes that also impact many suburban residents.

That is unlikely to happen in the Trump administration. Trump is committed to eviscerating the Department of Housing and Urban Development. His HUD secretary, Ben Carson, a neurosurgeon with no housing or economic-development experience whatsoever, has denounced federal housing assistance as "socialist," critiqued HUD's longstanding mandate to "affirmatively further fair housing" as meddling, and called on poor people to solve urban problems themselves.

Trump named Lynne Patton, his son Eric's wedding planner, to lead HUD's New York and New Jersey regional office, its largest. In one of her first official acts, she dropped a decade-long battle to desegregate housing in affluent Westchester County, New York. The GOP-led Congress recently approved a 2018 budget that axes nearly a half-billion dollars from HUD. Particularly hard hit will be HUD's program to provide rental assistance to low-income Americans, more than half of whom are elderly or disabled.

Trump's urban and housing policies (or their lack) will only worsen metropolitan inequality. They will make the lives of the poor even more insecure while also enriching the financiers, developers, and landlords whose reckless decisions brought the country to financial ruin.

Some three decades ago, just as Donald Trump was remaking parts of New York in his image, the urban geographer David Harvey described the city as "the high point of human achievement, objectifying the most sophisticated knowledge in a physical land-scape of extraordinary complexity, power, and splendor at the same time as it brings together social forces capable of the most amazing sociotechnical and political innovation. But it is also the site of squalid human failure, the lightning rod of the profound-est human discontents, and the arena of social and political con-flict." Trump's policies risk worsening that human failure and exacerbating that social and political conflict.

But some places are fighting back. Many municipalities, among them Baltimore, Boston, Chicago, Dallas, Denver, New Orleans, and Philadelphia, have been revitalized by an influx of Latin American immigrants and have declared themselves "sanctuary cities," resisting the Trump administration's efforts to use their scarce municipal resources to crack down on the undocumented.

New York's housing department has stepped up its efforts to require developers to set aside affordable housing for low- and middle-income residents. The new mayor of Jackson, Missis-sippi, Chokwe Antar Lumumba, is channeling resources to neigh-borhoods that have been ignored in service of flashy downtown redevelopment schemes. And Los Angeles has begun addressing its massive homelessness problem by setting aside nearly a billion dollars to provide long-term housing alternatives to shelters and living on the streets. Suburban school districts such as Norris-town, Pennsylvania, and Morristown, New Jersey, are creatively adapting their curricula and counseling to deal with an influx of new poor and working-class residents.

Municipal governments cannot solve the problems of inequal-ity, discrimination, and inadequate education and housing on their own. But in the Trump era, perhaps they can at least lay the groundwork for a more just and equitable urban policy in a post-Trump future.

THE MISINFORMATION SOCIETY

VICTOR PICKARD

rump's election laid bare structural flaws in our news and information systems. As mainstream news media sensationalized and trivialized what was at stake in the elections, social media amplified misinformation and propaganda. These media pathologies paved the way for the triumph of a demagogue. While criticism of such problems has escalated since the election, the underlying policies that enabled them have largely escaped scrutiny.

Policy decisions and indecisions have degraded our media environment over time and created what might be termed a "misinformation society." Some of the more pronounced features of the misinformation society are a lack of financial support for accountability journalism, the dominance of infrastructures of misinformation (i.e., the "Facebook problem"), and regulatory capture—whereby agencies harmonize their actions to serve the commercial interests of the very businesses they purportedly regulate—at the Federal Communications Commission, which is facilitating the concentration of media ownership by a handful of corporations and repealed the crucial internet protection of net neutrality.

How Did We Get Here?

These media failures weren't inevitable. Explicit policies favoring commercial interests over democratic concerns created this system. Unlike its counterparts around the world, the United States never developed a strong public-media sector, and it remains unique among democracies in its underfunding of public broadcasting—the United States today spends only about the price of a latte per capita per year on public media institutions. By comparison, Canada spends over thirty dollars per person, and northern European countries spend over one hundred dollars per person.[1]

Long under the sway of a corporate libertarian paradigm, the United States lacks a policy discourse that's sufficiently responsive to what I call "systemic market failure" in commercial media systems. This failure is characterized by the underproduction of public goods, such as quality news and information, which typically are not supported by the market.[2]

American media reformers have long fought for social-democratic alternatives that don't rely entirely on markets. But these efforts have often been derailed by a combination of red baiting, technocratic policy making, First Amendment absolutism, and, most of all, a commitment to market fundamentalism. The United States has therefore never developed a media-regulatory apparatus that could effectively counteract corporate power and commercial excesses.

Today, symptoms of extreme—and largely unregulated—commercialism in our media system include the ubiquity of clickbait, sponsored content, behavioral advertising, and corporate surveillance in our digital news media, along with a tendency toward media monopolies, a lack of public access to high-quality information, a loss of diverse voices and viewpoints, and the evisceration of public service journalism.

A Supply-Side Problem

A diminished supply of reliable news media is a core contributor to the misinformation society. Traditional newspapers—still the main source of original reporting for the American news media system—are gradually collapsing as both audiences and advertisers move online. Thus far, few news organizations have been able to monetize their online content in any significant way.

This means less revenue and fewer journalists. The number of news workers within the industry has plummeted, dropping by around 40 percent in the past decade. This erosion creates "news deserts," with entire regions going uncovered. Despite a post-election "Trump bump" in subscriptions for many publications, the drops in circulation, ad revenue, and number of news workers will likely continue in the coming years for the vast majority of newspapers.

In 2016 the Pew Research Center put this situation in stark relief, stating that "this accelerating decline suggests the industry may be past its point of no return."[3] Yet so far no public-policy response has emerged to deal with this crisis. Instead, most discussions about the journalism crisis focus on its symptoms, not its core problems. Because American journalism has depended on advertising revenue (with news as a by-product of the main transaction) for so long, this funding model is often taken to be the natural order of things, with alternatives falling outside of the political imaginary. It's long past time to champion noncommercial methods for nurturing a free and adversarial press. Fortunately some other models, such as that of *ProPublica*, which relies on a mix of grants and donations from philanthropic institutions and individuals, are beginning to emerge, but we need more. Without public-service journalism, democracy itself becomes dangerously vulnerable to a debased media culture of misinformation.

The Facebook Problem

A second broad policy problem is the Facebook-enabled misinformation infrastructure that threatens democratic discourse and elections around the globe. Beyond surface appearances, in reality Facebook is an algorithm-driven advertising company governed solely by profit imperatives. For its more than two billion users, it yields tremendous gatekeeping power over the distribution and presentation of information. Americans in particular are increasingly accessing news on Facebook, providing an opening for anonymous propagandists and foreign governments to interfere in U.S. elections.

Such profound media power residing in one monopolistic platform arguably presents a unique threat. A continual stream of revelations about Facebook's failure to prevent the spread of misinformation and protect users' privacy have caused a sea change in attitudes about whether the company's unchecked dominance is a policy problem. Facebook's sweeping power also is increasingly seen as a potential antitrust issue. According to the digital-publishing-analytics company Parse.ly, by the end of 2016, 42 percent of referral traffic to publisher sites came from Facebook. Facebook commands 77 percent of the mobile social-networking traffic in the United States; half of all American adults access its platform on a daily basis; and nearly all new digital-ad revenue is captured by it and Google.[4] It's tragically ironic that Facebook expects struggling news organizations to help stop the spread of fake news while it cuts off much of their economic sustenance.

If consensus continues to crystallize around the idea that Facebook is abusing its monopoly power and represents a serious threat to democracy, a number of potential policy interventions will come into focus. While other countries are increasingly disciplining Facebook with fines, we are starting to see some arguments for structural interventions within the United States, including breaking up the company—or at least having it divest itself of components such as WhatsApp, Messenger, and Instagram. Users' privacy protections and advertising regulations are other policy levers that might be considered as Facebook comes under increased scrutiny and governments try to curb its power.

Despite the public outcry, Facebook has done remarkably little to address these problems beyond calling on its user base to fact-check articles and report those of dubious veracity and by tweaking its algorithms.[5] More recently the company has hired additional human screeners and pledged greater transparency behind its ad-buying practices. Nonetheless, Facebook has so far shirked the traditional social responsibilities—lacking as they often are—of news-media publishers within a democratic society. Mark Zuckerberg has famously asserted that Facebook is a tech company, not a media company, and Sheryl Sandberg, Facebook's chief operating officer, reiterated this absurdity.

But although emphasizing Facebook's culpability is important, this problem is too large for the company to handle alone. It's the entire world's problem, which is why Facebook needs international regulatory oversight. Democratic societies must individually and collectively decide on Facebook's responsibilities and how they should be enforced. Self-regulation isn't sufficient.

At the very least, an independent press council of technologists, editors, and public advocates should be assembled to help monitor Facebook's actions and pressure it to be transparent and accountable. The governance of such a council must be determined publicly and internationally, with diverse constituencies participating in a bottom-up process.[6]

Trump's FCC

It may seem like Trump's pseudo-populist agenda, absent major legislative victories, has stalled. But while media attention is focused on Trump's latest tweets, his appointees are inflicting real damage at regulatory agencies, where a virulently pro-business agenda has slipped its leash to run roughshod over society's interests.

The FCC is exhibit A for this ideological agenda. Immediately upon assuming control, FCC chairman Ajit Pai sought to jettison net neutrality and other internet safeguards and has moved quickly to loosen media-ownership regulations, giving internet service providers and media corporations even more power. Under Pai's leadership, the FCC's policy changes have been tailor-made to benefit companies like Sinclair Broadcast Group, the largest television station owner in the United States. Sinclair is well known for airing right-wing content (such as the notorious 2004 documentary *Stolen Honor*, which attacked then–Democratic presidential nominee John Kerry's Vietnam War record) and for requiring its local stations to run conservative commentaries. The FCC has even rewritten rules to allow media outlets like Sinclair to obscure their actual market share, and it has green-lighted various megamergers and repealed cross-ownership bans in local news markets, which may hasten the rise of one-newsroom towns.

Market libertarians typically rationalize these interventions as freeing industry from heavy-handed governmental interference in the name of "deregulation." A more accurate term for this pro-industry agenda, however, is *reregulation*. Such an agenda requires aggressive government intervention aimed at restructuring media systems to benefit corporate interests instead of the public. Accordingly, Chairman Pai is rushing to satisfy cable and phone companies' long-standing policy wish lists.

Ultimately, these moves signal a textbook definition of regulatory capture. This abuse of power is exemplified by the FCC's plan to scrap net neutrality protections, which would allow internet service providers like Comcast and Verizon to limit our access to online content, censor particular forms of speech, and create pay-to-play "fast lanes" that would further amplify corporate power. But until we address the larger threat of unregulated monopoly power, we can't address infrastructure problems stemming from the lack of competition in internet-service markets, such as outrageously high costs, slow speeds, and digital redlining (not providing broadband access to poorer communities that are outside of profitable areas).

What's to Be Done?

The ongoing failures of the commercial media system are deeply structural, and remedying them will require structural reforms. However, discourses about the democratic potential of digital technologies often overlook the policy roots and normative foundations of our communication systems. An abiding faith in technological liberation and a tendency to naturalize market forces have discouraged the implementation of public policies that could prevent corporate capture of our core information systems.

This discursive orientation at least partly explains why American society ever allowed platform monopolies such as Facebook to obtain such tremendous and unaccountable power in the first place. It also helps explain the meager policy responses to our ongoing journalism crisis. The degraded media system resulting from these policy failures created a fertile landscape for various kinds of misinformation to thrive.

The first steps we take toward addressing these policy problems must be discursive. Articulating that our news media are public services and infrastructures—not simply commodities—is an essential starting point. Additionally, we must be adamant that the market can't provide for all our information needs. Shifting the media-regulatory paradigm from corporate libertarianism to social democracy would help facilitate policies that reduce monopoly power, remove commercial pressures, install public-interest protections, and build out public alternatives.

Although we can work at the state and local levels to build things like municipal broadband services, few other elements of this program are politically possible in the United States right now. But it's precisely during dark political moments like this one that we should plan for—and help create—a more enlightened future. The policy interventions enumerated above may not sit comfortably with those more inclined to let technology companies and the market decide for us how our communication systems should be designed. But we no longer have that luxury (if we ever did). The commercialization and corporate monopolization of our news and information systems are significant social problems. They fall within the realm of policy and, therefore, politics.

There is, of course, no easy fix. In the short term, popular pressures must be exerted on multiple fronts, ranging from calls to the FCC and Congress to financial support of opposition journalism. Confronting misinformation requires a diversity of tactics. While it's not feasible to bring back content regulations like the long-repealed Fairness Doctrine, demanding more social responsibility from major media institutions, especially Facebook, is key. And finding ways to structurally support actual journalism is even more essential. For example, the philanthropy world should redouble efforts to shore up—and reinvent—struggling newspapers as they transition to nonprofit status.

A longer-term agenda should be more ambitious. We need to envision a media system not beholden to monopoly power and extreme commercialism. This means breaking up media conglomerates and oligopolies or, where they're deemed "natural monopolies," heavily regulating them. Tim Wu suggested in a piece for the *New York Times* that we encourage Facebook to become a public-benefit corporation for which profit is no longer the sole purpose.

For the long term we must also establish true public alternatives not dependent on the market—ideally a new public-service media system supported through a combination of private contributions and public subsidies (which is how the original PBS system took root).[7] One intriguing idea is a proposal put forth by British reformers for Facebook and Google to allocate a small percentage of their advertising revenue—which could generate many millions of dollars—toward public-service journalism.

If we're to grant monopolies such incredible power over our vital communication infrastructures, we'll need a new social contract. By regulating these giants and creating public alternatives, we just might create a media system in service to democracy, not to the misinformation society.

NOTES

Revised June 25, 2018

1. Rodney Benson and Matt Powers, "Public Media and Political Independence: Lessons for the Future of Journalism from Around the World," *Free Press*, February 10, 2011, https://www.freepress.net/blog/11/02/10/public-media-and-political-independence-lessons-future-journalism-around-world.

2. For a chronicle of the history of this market failure, see Victor Pickard, *America's Battle for Media Democracy* (Cambridge: Cambridge University Press, 2014).

3. Michael Barthel, "Five Key Takeaways about the State of the News Media in 2016," Pew Research Center, June 15, 2016, http://www.pewresearch.org/fact-tank/2016/06/15/state-of-the-news-media-2016-key-takeaways/.

4. Craig Silverman, "This Analysis Shows How Fake Election News Stories Outperformed Real News on Facebook," *BuzzFeed*, November 16, 2016, https://www.buzzfeed.com/craigsilverman/viral-fake-election-news-outperformed-real-news-on-facebook.

5. Barry Lynn and Matt Stoller, "How to Stop Google and Facebook from Becoming Even More Powerful," *Guardian*, November 2, 2017, https://www.theguardian.com/commentisfree/2017/nov/02/facebook-google-monopoly-companies.

6. See, for example, Adam Mosseri, "Working to Stop Misinformation and False News," FaceBook Newsroom, April 6, 2017.

7. Victor Pickard, "A Social Democratic Vision of Media: Toward a Radical Pre-history of Public Broadcasting," *Journal of Radio and Audio Media* 24, no. 2 (2017): 200–212.

DEFENDING OPEN CITIES

SASKIA SASSEN

Cities have distinctive capacities to transform conflict into the civic. In contrast, national governments tend to militarize conflict. This does not mean that cities are peaceful spaces. On the contrary, cities have long been sites of conflict, from wars between nations to wars between classes, as well as sites of racism and religious hatred, expressed through rioting, pogroms, and the like. While war can install itself in cities, the militarizing of conflict is not, in principle, a particularly urban mode. Tanks and armored vehicles do not belong in cities.

And yet increasingly militarization *is* taking root in the daily life of our cities, in the shape of police forces with advanced military equipment and of crowd-control strategies that more than slightly resemble those employed in overseas battle zones. This trend has been building for the last two decades or more, at least from the time of the anti-WTO protests of the 1990s; it is manifest today in everything from how the police respond to large-scale protests such as those of Black Lives Matter to how SWAT teams and tactics are used to storm houses and apartment blocks in pursuit of gang members and drug dealers. We are now seeing it play out in the cat-and-mouse games between undocumented immigrants and increasingly assertive ICE agents.

Much of this isn't new. But under Trump, as he plays an updated version of Nixon's "silent majority" law-and-order game, urban militarization seems to be gaining a peculiar kind of legitimacy, morphing into ever more extreme forms in the process.

We see this in the renewed push to get army surplus gear to police—a policy that began under Bill Clinton but that Obama at least tried to rein in somewhat. We see it in Trump's calling on police "not to be too gentle" with suspects, in Attorney General Sessions's rolling back of civil-rights investigations of police brutality and calls for a reinvigorated war on drugs and for prosecutors to pursue the most serious charges they possibly can in criminal cases and more. We see it in legislative and fiscal attacks on sanctuary cities—some of these attacks emanating from the feds, others from conservative state governments in Texas and elsewhere.

We see it too, of course, in this administration's willingness to talk aloud about unleashing nuclear weapons against North Korea's cities and in the implication that it might also be prepared to unleash carnage against the cities of other purportedly hostile nations, including Iran and Venezuela. A generation after the Cold War ended, Trump's military strategy seems to be strikingly similar to that of the dark days of mutually assured destruction—the promise to turn enemy cities into radioactive wastelands, with the hope that the rhetoric is savage enough to deflect the actual realization of such acts.

The City: A Space with Civic Potentials

While cities have frequently been sites of violence and upheaval, they have also worked out how to avoid such violence most of the time: the urban mode is to triage conflict through commerce and civic activity. Even more important, the overcoming of urban conflicts has often been the source of an expanded civic sense. For instance, the arrival of large numbers of immigrants in Europe's major cities in the early 1900s had the ironic effect of strengthening public services. Let me illustrate. When the numbers of users became massive, local governments could not demand a demonstration of national identity to access public transport. A simple token—the ticket, the coin—had to suffice. We can repeat this across several public services: when the numbers become massive, the system needs to simplify controls and thereby expand access.

The many worlds contained in a city enable residents to be a variety of subjects, to occupy a whole host of disparate identities simultaneously. In a mine or a factory or an office, the worker is controlled and managed. In a public transport system she is not a firm's "worker"; she is a passenger. Nor is she the firm's worker when she goes out for lunch; she becomes a customer. We can repeat this for all kinds of situations in a city. In short, the many worlds contained in a city enable its residents to wear many hats.

At their best, the daily dynamics and interdependencies of life in the city contribute to the making of an *urban* subject, as distinct from an ethnic, religious, or racialized subject. Being an urban subject is a temporary condition, but it matters profoundly for a city. Most of the time, in most moments of history, in most geographic locales, humans are specific subjects marked by ethnicity, language, phenotype, and more. But in the vortex of a modern, complex city's daily transactions we all become urban subjects.

I think of the possibility of an *urban* subject not as one that erases the powerful markers of difference in a city, but as one that repositions those differences, even if only for a while, and that thereby can contribute to sociability. This repositioning is likely to take on many diverse forms and involve diverse spaces, depending on the city: public transport, car cultures, the subway, public spaces, large office atriums, lunch counters, hospitals, and so on. The late afternoon subway rush is full of enormously diverse types of workers—from cleaners to executives: but in that moment, they are all urban subjects.

Are Today's Cities Losing Their Role as Civic Ground?

Today, many cities are at risk of losing this capacity for making urban subjects. Instead, as they stratify, they become both playgrounds for the rich and ghettos for the poor: sites for a range of new types of conflicts. It is no coincidence that in an age of vast inequalities we are seeing an upswing in abusive police actions, as well as class war and a resurgence of older modes of ethnic and social "cleansing."

Dense urban spaces can easily become conflictive spaces in cities overwhelmed by inequality and injustice. Add to this the major environmental disasters looming in our immediate futures that will hit the poor particularly hard, and we can see how our major cities could easily become sites for a variety of secondary, more anomic conflicts, ones that go beyond the more familiar conflicts we have long seen in U.S. cities.

All of this challenges the traditional commercial and civic capacity that has given cities tools to avoid falling into armed conflict and to incorporate diversities of class, culture, religion, ethnicity. It leads to walled-in communities, whether the walls are material or imagined, to cities made up of tribes and clans.

Are the current urban wars arising from racism, police abuse, and the militarizing of a growing number of police forces only going to get worse with the current Washington leadership? Brutality, lack of accountability, and a national government that is doing nothing to control these negative conditions: is this the new normal in our country? The evidence from the first year of the Trump presidency suggests this may well be the case. Trends that have been building for the last several decades—from police brutality to shrinking political support for the modest middle class—are now in full bloom.

In the twentieth century, both the modest social classes and the powerful found in the city a space for their diverse "life projects." None of these cities and projects were perfect. All of them contained strands of hatred and injustice. But the complex interdependence of daily life in cities was the algorithm that made them thrive.

This is no longer quite the case in today's major cities. We are seeing an unsettling of older urban orders. It is part of a larger disassembling of existing organizational logics and hence unlikely to produce urbanities that resemble those of our recent past. Think of all those newly built empty towers in midtown and now also lower Manhattan: they deurbanize the city. Similar growth patterns can be seen in London, in LA, and in a slew of other global cities. Prosperity begets rampant development—but not always of the kind that binds communities into tighter urban arrangements.

This disassembling is also unsettling the logic that assembled territory, authority, and rights into the dominant organizational format of our times—the modern nation-state. All of this is happening even as both cities and national states continue to be major building blocks of the current geopolitical landscape and the material organization of territory. In this sense, the urban order that gave us the open city is still there but increasingly merely as visual order and not as a social order that can enable the making of urban subjects.

These dynamics are altering the familiar urban order and generating extraordinary challenges. Confronting these challenges will require that we transcend our differences. Therein lies a potential for reinventing the capacity of cities to transform conflict into openness rather than war. But the result is not necessarily going to be the familiar order of decades past.

NOTE

This short paper is part of a larger project, "Ethics in the City," supported by the Kaifeng Foundation. See also, by the same author, *Expulsions: Brutality and Complexity in the Global Economy* (2014).

CRIMINALIZING IMMIGRANTS

ALINA DAS

Peering out the windows of John F. Kennedy Airport in the early morning hours of January 29, 2017, I had hope for this country's future on immigration policy. Hundreds of ordinary New Yorkers were still gathered outside the airport protesting the first iteration of President Trump's Muslim Ban. Inside the airport, desperate but resilient individuals awaited news of their loved ones who had been detained. A U.S. Army sergeant paced the terminal, concerned for his elderly mother, who should have been permitted to enter as a lawful permanent resident. A cluster of university students gathered at the security barricades, looking for their classmate to arrive to resume her school year. An expectant father held his face in his hands, anxious for his mother-in-law to be released while his pregnant wife waited for them both in the hospital.

Mixed among all of these people were lawyers and advocates filing emergency petitions and attempting to persuade U.S. Customs and Border Protection agents to comply with a federal court order, issued the previous day, that had put a temporary halt on the ban. As we settled in that evening to await daybreak and the hoped-for release of those detained, I could not help but admire the people inside and out of the airport who were willing to speak out against these anti-immigrant policies. President Trump's "America First" platform somehow did not include us, but we were not willing to cede the American Dream to his discriminatory, anti-immigrant agenda.

A year after the 2016 election, it has become clear that the fight to protect immigrant rights will require us to sustain this high level of resiliency and advocacy for years to come as President Trump's anti-immigrant net widens. Each of Trump's executive orders and pronouncements on immigration plays dangerously on powerful anti-immigrant themes. The Muslim Ban, first introduced as "Protecting the Nation from Foreign Terrorist Entry into the United States," and reformulated several times since, relies on the idea that immigrants and refugees are terrorists.

Two other early executive orders, "Enhancing Public Safety in the Interior of the United States" and "Border Security and Immigration Enforcement Improvements," treat immigrants and refugees as criminals. Most recently, the threats to Temporary Protected Status for over 300,000 immigrants who left countries decimated by civil conflict and natural disasters, and Attorney General Jeff Sessions's announcement of the end of Deferred Action for Childhood Arrivals (DACA), the popular Obama-era program that granted nearly 800,000 young immigrants a temporary reprieve from the threat of deportation, have demonstrated that no group of immigrants is off-limits for President Trump's deportation machine.

The first and the last of the items on this long list of restrictionist moves—the Muslim Ban and the DACA rescission—have most captivated the public. These policy changes betray our core American values: the former by targeting people for their religious beliefs and abandoning our historic commitment to refugees and the latter by targeting young people who honored their end of the deal by giving the government their personal data and pursuing education and work opportunities only to once again face deportation. We must commit ourselves to the movements to end the Muslim Ban and to pass clean legislation that puts undocumented immigrants on a path to legal status without introducing additional draconian, anti-immigrant measures as collateral.[1]

But the middle set of executive actions—the ramping up of interior and border immigration enforcement—deserves equal attention and resistance from the immigrant-rights movement. President Trump is dramatically bulking up what was already a massive deportation machine, and we are particularly vulnerable to entrenchment on these issues where the targeted population can be labeled "criminal aliens" and "border security threats." After all, the Obama administration itself used these buzzwords to deport 3 million people from the United States while priding itself on its use of prosecutorial discretion to prevent deportation in some cases.[2]

President Trump has collapsed this limited system of prosecutorial discretion, expanding the notion of "criminal" to people with convictions no matter how minor or old and even to those whom immigration officials deem to have committed a chargeable criminal offense in cases where no charges have been filed. Trump supports these policies because, as he said using openly racist rhetoric, he wants to go after the "bad hombres."

As a law professor who studies the intersection of immigration and criminal law and as an immigrant-rights lawyer who defends the rights of all immigrants, I know how damning and disingenuous the divide between so-called good and bad immigrants is. The history of U.S. immigration policy is a history of eugenics, white supremacy, and racist exclusion.[3] The history of U.S. criminal legal policy is a history of racism, white supremacy, and the reformulation of slavery and Jim Crow.[4] Combining these systems—labeling someone a "criminal alien"—maximizes the flaws in both and has a disparate impact on communities of color.

We are beginning to understand, from the fight against the "War on Drugs," that associations of criminality and the accumulation of a criminal record often have more do to with race and class than a person's actions. We are also beginning to understand, through the movement to end mass incarceration, that harsh punishments cause more problems for our country than they solve.

So, too, does the double punishment of deporting someone after they have already paid their debt to society for an old conviction. I know this because it is the lesson that people who have faced deportation as so-called criminal aliens have taught me. People like Warren Hilarion Joseph—a decorated Gulf War veteran and green card holder who was detained for over three years and almost deported for an old conviction for which he had already paid his debt to society.[5] Only a lengthy legal battle—for which he had to rely on pro bono support and community resources since there is no right to government-appointed counsel in such cases—prevented his deportation. Our government incarcerated him and sought to separate him permanently from his U.S.-citizen children. Why? What purpose would his deportation have served? What explanation would we have given his American children? Shouldn't "America First" include them, too?

I was reminded of the hypocrisy of the Trump administration's arguments most recently at the start of the Supreme Court term, when our justices heard oral arguments in *Jennings v. Rodriguez*, a case that will decide whether immigrants like Mr. Joseph should have the simple right to a bail hearing while they fight their deportation cases.[6] The attorney for the Trump administration argued that immigrants have no constitutional right to a hearing about the government's justification for their detention. Indeed, he blamed immigrants for their own detention, asserting that the "alien always has the option of terminating the detention by accepting a final order of removal and returning home."[7]

As an attorney for the ACLU pointed out in response, home *is* America for many of the immigrants who are detained and facing deportation—including the lead plaintiff in the case, Alejandro Rodriguez, who came to the United States as a one-year-old. Yet, to the Trump administration, immigrants are perpetual foreigners and law-breakers, undeserving of constitutional protections.

It should come as little surprise that President Trump wants to use every tool in his arsenal—starting with riffs on "criminal aliens" and "terrorists"—to defend a vast expansion of the detention and deportation system. He has singlehandedly revived the private-prison industry, a major financial contributor to his campaign. Private-prison corporations run 65 percent of immigration prisons while another 25 percent are run through lucrative contracts with county jails.[8]

In the waning days of the Obama administration, the Department of Justice announced that the Bureau of Prisons would begin phasing out its use of private prisons. An investigation was also conducted by the Homeland Security Advisory Council, which voted to move away from reliance on private prisons and county jails in the immigration-detention context. These positions were reversed by the Trump administration within weeks of his inauguration, and as a result the stock prices for private prison companies have skyrocketed.[9]

We see this mentality reflected in the Trump administration's most recent "principles" for immigration reform.[10] In the name of fighting crime, Trump, advised by hardliners like Stephen Miller, has proposed policies that would put thousands of additional immigration officers on our streets and in our communities;

financially punish cities and towns that seek to protect immigrants from the harms of our broken immigration system; build a wall around this country; expand policies to incarcerate those who cross our borders; and divide families and communities within our borders, too. These are the policies—targeted at "criminal aliens" and "border threats"—where we have the most to lose because for the most part they have been supported by Democratic and Republican administrations alike, allowing the immigration detention and deportation system to flourish and expand even as political winds change.

Just as people gathered on the streets to protest the Muslim Ban and the rescission of DACA, so too must we hold steadfast against the expansion of our immigration-enforcement machinery. President Trump has managed to collapse U.S. immigrant-enforcement priorities for deportation into one large category that includes virtually every immigrant. So we, too, must include every immigrant in our vision of immigrant justice. Only an inclusive approach will allow us to move past the current hateful rhetoric of division and refocus immigration policy on human dignity, due process, and respect for all people.

NOTES

1. Many community organizations are mobilizing against these policies. Learn more at No Muslim Ban Ever (https://www.nomuslimbanever.com/) and United We Dream (http://weareheretostay.org/).

2. If "returns" are included in addition to formal removals, the number of people targeted by President Obama jumps to 5 million. See Muzaffar Chishti, Sarah Pierce, and Jessica Bolter, "The Obama Record on Deportations: Deporter in Chief or Not?," Migration Policy Institute, January 26, 2017, https://www.migrationpolicy.org/article/obama-record -deportations-deporter-chief-or-not.

3. See Ian Henry López, *White by Law: The Legal Construction of Race* (New York: New York University Press, 1996); Mae M. Ngai, *Impossible Subjects:*

Illegal Aliens and the Making of Modern America (Princeton, NJ: Princeton University Press, 2004); Alina Das, "Inclusive Immigrant Justice: Racial Animus and the Origins of Crime-Based Deportation," *UC Davis Law Review* 52, no. 1 (November 2018): 171–96, https://papers.ssrn .com/sol3/papers.cfm?abstract_id=3064940.

4. See Michelle Alexander, *The New Jim Crow: Mass Incarceration in the Age of Colorblindness* (New York: The New Press, 2010).

5. Learn more about Mr. Joseph's story from Human Rights Watch: https:// www.hrw.org/video-photos/video/2014/07/17/torn-apart-hilarion -warren-joseph.

6. Prolonged immigration detention destroys the lives of many American families. For a window into the real-life impact of detention, visit Prolonged Detention Stories (http://www.prolongeddetentionstories.org/).

7. Transcript of Oral Arguments, Jennings v. Rodriguez, No. 15-1204 (Sup. Ct. Oct. 3, 2017), 25, https://www.supremecourt.gov/oral_arguments /argument_transcripts/2017/15-1204_m6hn.pdf.

8. See U.S. Department of Homeland Security, Homeland Security Advisory Council, "Report of the Subcommittee on Privatized Immigration Detention Facilities 6" (2016), https://www.dhs.gov/sites/default/files /publications/DHS%2520HSAC%2520PIDF%2520Final%2520Report.pdf.

9. Editorial, "Under Trump, Private Prisons Thrive Again," *New York Times*, February 24, 2017, https://www.nytimes.com/2017/02/24/opinion/under -mr-trump-private-prisons-thrive-again.html.

10. President Donald J. Trump's Letter to House and Senate Leaders and Immigration Principles and Policies, October 8, 2017, https://www .whitehouse.gov/the-press-office/2017/10/08/president-donald-j-trumps -letter-house-and-senate-leaders-immigration.

TRUMP, TRADE, AND WAR

OONA A. HATHAWAY AND SCOTT J. SHAPIRO

President Trump has proven to be a reckless leader. His refusal to denounce white supremacists, his repeated attacks on journalists and free speech, his courting of Vladimir Putin, his attempts to belittle and provoke the North Korean leader—every single one of these acts is corrosive and destabilizing. While the media has understandably focused on the risks of authoritarianism and nuclear war, there is another grave danger that has largely gone unnoticed: President Trump's rejection of free trade.

It may take years before historians fully understand why President Trump won the election. But already we know that his message resonated with an electorate that had suffered from economic dislocation and growing inequality and that was tired of what has been called a "forever war." Trump promised a new America, an America that put itself (or at least certain parts of itself) first. To the candidate and his electorate, our seventy years of global order were, at best, outdated. As his campaign progressed, Trump began hawking an international agenda built on two pillars: protectionism and isolationism. In a nod to the isolationists and pro-fascists of 1930s America, he even began referring to this agenda as "America First."

During the 2016 campaign, Donald Trump attacked free trade, promising to erect tariffs and barriers to keep manufacturing and jobs at home, to withdraw from negotiations over the Trans-Pacific Partnership, to renegotiate NAFTA, and to punish China for devaluing its currency.

Trump's critics pointed out many problems with his protectionist positions: protectionism is economically inefficient; it is an assault on the post–World War Two American conception of freedom and liberty; it is a futile fight against globalization—a stance that has been proven, time and again, to be on the wrong side of history. Trump's isolationism is a retreat from America's role in world affairs and will lead to global instability; a declaration of defeat in the global war on terror; and an abdication of America's decades-long policy of spreading democracy and protecting human rights.

But the critics missed the biggest problem with Trump's embrace of protectionism: trade today plays the role in the world order that war once played. Trade gives states a way to influence one another without resorting to force, as was once common. Giving up on trade means giving up on that influence, leaving states with little choice but war.

To understand why this is the case, one has to return to what we have described as the "Old World Order." For hundreds of years, waging war was considered a necessary function to run a state. As described and systematized by the so-called father of international law, Hugo Grotius in the early seventeenth century, international law permitted states to use force in order to right (perceived or otherwise) wrongs. Actually, it did more than permit war. The system *relied on war* as a tool of international justice. It was the way in which states collected unpaid debts, obtained compensation for wrongful harms, enforced treaty obligations, and protected religious interests, among much else.

In this world, war to enforce legal rights was perfectly legal but economic sanctions by neutrals against belligerents were *illegal*. Neutrals had a duty of impartiality in a conflict—states outside of a conflict could not offer more favorable trade terms to the state it favored. To do so was illegal and would give the disfavored state a cause for war.

As we argue in our recent book, *The Internationalists: How a Radical Plan to Outlaw War Remade the World*, that all changed in 1928. Over sixty countries ratified the Kellogg-Briand Pact (also known as the Peace Pact). By outlawing war, the Peace Pact changed the role of war in the international system. War could no longer legally be used between states to resolve disputes, to right wrongs, or to force uncooperative states to cooperate.

The pact did not work overnight, of course. As we show in the book, it took decades to figure out how to make the promise of the pact a reality. One of the crucial moments came shortly after it entered into force: in 1931, Japan, which was a party to the agreement, committed a clear violation by invading Manchuria. The world was unsure how to respond: surely it could not enforce the prohibition on war with war. But if not war, then what?

The answer came when U.S. secretary of state Henry Stimson wrote to Japan and China on January 8, 1932: "The American Government . . . does not intend to recognize any situation, treaty, or agreement which may be brought about by means contrary to the covenants and obligations of the Pact of Paris"—another name for the Kellogg-Briand Pact. The League of Nations quickly followed suit. The doctrine of nonrecognition would become known as the "Stimson Doctrine" and would give rise to a new way to enforce the law: not with war but with so-called sanctions of peace. As Stimson explained in a speech entitled "The Pact of Paris: Three Year Later," the pact had set in motion a change in the laws of neutrality, which for the first time permitted states to put in place economic sanctions against parties to a war, using trade, not force, as a way to enforce the law.

Economic sanctions thus slowly began to fill the void left by the decision to outlaw war. They became one of the most powerful weapons a country could wield. By placing sanctions on uncooperative nations, the international community could effect change without violence. States could no longer use war to enforce the law, but they could use sanctions to "outcast" misbehaving states.

To see how sanctions can be used as a substitute for war, consider the events that led to the Iran nuclear deal. In 2006, the UN Security Council joined the United States in economically isolating Iran. It demanded that Iran stop uranium enrichment and imposed progressively more painful trade sanctions in response to its continued intransigence. As a result, Iran was shut out of global commerce not only by the United States and a few sympathetic countries but by nearly every nation in the world.

The sanctions regime was further tightened in 2010 by an obscure office in the U.S. Treasury Department: the Office of Foreign Asset Control, or OFAC. At the behest of OFAC, Congress passed the Comprehensive Iran Sanctions, Accountability, and Divestment Act, which strengthened U.S. sanctions on the Iranian energy industry and financial sector. Whereas previous measures had targeted only Iranian firms, Congress now authorized the imposition of "secondary sanctions" on any bank, anywhere in the world, that transacted with Iran's central bank. Any bank placed on the blacklist could be cut off from access to the U.S. financial sector. The United States offered banks a choice: you can do business with the United States or you can do business with Iran; you can't do both.

These sanctions worked remarkably well: Iran's oil exports fell by more than 50 percent; the value of the nation's currency (the rial) plummeted; and in 2012, Iran's economy shrunk by about

7 percent, prompting Iranian president Mahmoud Ahmadinejad to complain: "The enemy has announced that it has imposed sanctions. . . . This is a hidden war. A broad and heavy war, spread across the globe."

Ahmadinejad's statement was evidence that the sanctions were imposing costs. But as David Cohen, the Treasury official who oversaw OFAC, pointed out, the sanctions were not a secret war. They were instead "done for all the world to see" and, indeed, "done by all the world." Nor were they actually a war, Cohen continued, but "the alternative to war." And that alternative worked.

In August 2013, Hassan Rouhani succeeded President Ahmadinejad after running on a platform of improving relations with the rest of the world and sanctions relief. The new Iranian leadership began negotiations with the "P5 plus one"—the permanent five members of the Security Council plus Germany, the economic steward of the EU. In November 2013, they reached an interim agreement limiting Iran's nuclear program and partially lifting sanctions and made plans to complete a more permanent, comprehensive agreement. For the first time in decades, there was real hope that a nuclear Iran could be prevented through discussions at the negotiating table rather than with military strikes.

Now President Trump, by calling into question the U.S. commitment to free trade and global economic integration, is threatening to unilaterally disarm. The less business it does with the rest of the world, the less influence it will have in the modern legal order. Raising trade barriers and withdrawing from free trade agreements mean giving up power and influence.

The president's twin messages of isolationism and protectionism are dangerous. If the U.S. pulls back from unilateral trade and cooperation, it will be left with fewer diplomatic options. States that outcast themselves find it difficult to outcast other nations. What's more, giving up the capacity to influence states through trade can cause states to look longingly at the Old World Order tool of influence: war.

North Korea is an excellent example of a country caught in this trap. It is so isolated from the global economy that it has little influence over other states other than the threat of military force. Its capacity to exert influence outside its borders depends entirely on its nuclear weapons program; it has nothing else.

Indeed, even as Trump has been threatening to withdraw from free trade arrangements, he has been relying more heavily on the military to get what he wants. He has doubled-down on virtually every American military engagement. He has sent U.S. troops into Syria to assist the fight against ISIS. He has stepped up support for the Saudi-led fight in Yemen, even in the face of reported war crimes. He has fired missiles in retaliation for Syrian chemical weapons attacks.

In September, Trump announced that he is sending more U.S. troops into Afghanistan. He has loosened the rules of engagement in Afghanistan as well. He has even suggested that he might use the U.S. military in Venezuela. In front of the United Nations, the home of peaceful cooperation, he threatened to "totally destroy" North Korea, implying his willingness to use weapons against millions of civilians. And, most recently, Trump has refused to certify part of the Iran nuclear deal, raising the specter that the deal will break down and Trump will ultimately resort to military force against Iran.

The lesson Trump has yet to learn is that in the modern era trade is more than trade. Trade is the power to exert peaceful and effective influence abroad. Giving up on trade means walking away from that influence. "America First" threatens to put America last, at least on the international stage.

Trump's lasting legacy may be even more destabilizing than the most dire predictions issued at the start of his presidency. By pulling back American support for free trade, Trump threatens America's nearly century-long run of being the "indispensable nation." Even after he leaves office, that lesson will linger. For decades, the U.S. dollar has been the foundation of the world's economy; countries have freely lent to the United States; and English has been the dominant language on the international stage. If the United States relinquishes its leadership role, we should wonder: who will fill the void we leave behind?

RULE BY MISRULE

RICHARD SENNETT

osters declaring "No Trump, no KKK, no Fascist USA!" and the like feature in most anti-Trump rallies. Viscerally, it's clear what the posters mean: no more threats to children of illegal immigrants, no more sympathy for white supremacists . . . but the placards do not convey that something more is at stake in the leader's behavior than being vicious minded.

Trump is not a fascist in the sense Mussolini was; he is not a control freak micromanaging the levers of government. He is not an ideological fascist hewing to a single set of beliefs, no matter what. Yesterday, he was going to build thousands of miles of impermeable wall against the Mexican hordes; today, he says, the wall will come sometime "later." Once a Republican, now he now plays footsie with Democrats. And Trump is not a fascist in the sense Geert Wilders of the Netherlands is, a politician who tries to convince the eminently practical Dutch that it's just good common sense to hate and expel Muslims. Yes, in public Trump is always blindly angry at something and sneering at someone, but most of all he is a master at manipulating instability—his own and others.

So why is it that so many think Trump is not simply nasty but, in a meaningful way, in a way different from that of other unpleasant American politicians who have come before him, actually a fascistic personality type in charge of what is becoming an at least partially fascistic governing apparatus?

This public persona is not detached from a certain kind of government practice. In fascist structures historically, the leader demands absolute, slavish loyalty from those below, bureaucrats obeying orders precisely and unthinkingly. Mussolini famously sought to make the trains in Italy run on time, no matter whether train conductors and engine operators were good fascists or not: he decreed this would happen, and his minions would make it happen—or else. Hannah Arendt argued that this state-machine produced the "banality of evil," as in the Nazi death camps, where the killers claimed they were just following orders and where "ordinary" people could willingly perform unimaginably cruel acts at the urging of charismatic leaders and a corrupted bureaucratic state. The state shows the same rigid face in George Orwell's *1984* or in Dave Eggers's tech dystopia, *The Circle*. Mussolini called this kind of state "Fascism's call to Order."

In the Trump sort of fascist regime, the leader traumatizes those who serve him by keeping them off balance. He knows that changing his mind on a whim, being unpredictable or contradictory, will focus those serving him obsessively on trying to fathom what he wants—today. They try to appease him or please him but aren't certain how. You can see this sort of keep-them-off-balance tyranny at work in many family firms, when ruled by a patriarch setting the junior family members against one another, each trying to curry personal favor. Trump ran his real-estate empire along these lines, the firm constantly turning and twisting, executives never certain where they were with him. Trump has now transferred this way of "leading" to Washington. He is firming up despotic personal power by destabilizing the state. Far from being out of his mind, as many commentators believe, I think that in this he is really clever. He rules by misrule.

In Washington, Steve Bannon has been Trump's guru for ruling this way. Bannon wants to deconstruct the administrative state, following the early Lenin's belief in causing as much governmental chaos as possible when a new regime comes to power. Cabinet posts filled by saboteurs of regulation or even, as with the current HUD housing regime, by self-confessed incompetents, serve the purpose. To be sure, the strategy—in Washington today as in Moscow a century ago—applies to the strategists as well. Bannon is gone. Flynn is gone. Priebus is gone.

In classic fascist systems, people in government who disobey the leader often wind up in jail or dead. In Trumpism, there are no such catastrophic penalties. People working for government may remain in place, but they are exiled into a sort of perpetual limbo. At the bottom levels of the American government, this has happened to workers in the environment and housing ministries.

Unfilled government posts are another tactic of rule by misrule. The American Department of State, which has played such a vital role in the accumulation of American global influence over the past century, has become a weak agency, unable to mount much institutional policy of its own because its personnel have been drastically reduced. Those who remain in posts abroad struggle to keep the doors open, issuing passports or notarizing documents rather than doing analysis. As in Trump's business, so in his government, good people with other options leave if they can. There are, to be sure, many dedicated people in the National Institutes of Health, the Forestry Service, the State Department, and HUD. But, with their skills devalued, there is less and less reason to stay; when they give up, rule by misrule is only strengthened.

A curious kind of Machiavellianism appears in rule by misrule. Betrayal and disloyalty become standard practice. The two glaring cases in Trump's regime concern the governor of New Jersey, Chris Christie, and the former mayor of New York, Rudy Giuliani:

early supporters pushed aside when Trump came to power, now supplicants to be let back inside the gates. Humiliation is also a potent weapon, as for Trump's former aide-de-camp Reince Priebus, whom Trump obliged to kill flies during meetings, or his hapless press spokesman Sean Spicer, deliberately prevented from meeting the pope during Trump's Vatican visit earlier this year.

Here there is a difference between Trump the businessman and Trump the president. Trump the businessman made so many enemies that no banks who had worked with him—save Deutsche Bank—would continue to put up with him. In office, in his immediate circle insult and humiliation carry no such practical consequences; no one seems to stand up to him publicly—witness the discomfort silently endured by several of his Jewish advisers as they stood on the podium with him while he said that some of the Nazis who marched in Charlottesville were "very fine people." Instead, they "interpret," they "explain," and so they excuse.

In this regard, Trump, is a narcissist of a peculiar sort. Bored by anything not related to himself, he is curiously sloppy, unable to pay attention to arguments or documents of more than a page— unlike the obsessive narcissists who would scan every last sentence to make sure it is what he wants. Trump's tweets serve this sort of narcissism-with-a-short-attention-span persona, conveying a momentary belief or feeling rather than a considered judgment.

Grinding bureaucracy or rule by misrule are not inherently fascist in operation. Government structures earn that term when they legitimate themselves by drawing on the politics of purge: evil forces—Jewish bankers, Mexican grape pickers, transgenders, political correctors, eco-ranters, etc.—all are weakening the economy, taking jobs away from "us," or sapping the moral fiber of the country. Fascism is puritanical in the sense that its adherents portray the world around them in black-and-white, good-and-evil terms. Antidemocratic policies follow directly from the puritan purge: rather than working with complexity, avoid it. As Richard Hofstadter long ago observed, the puritan-purge impulse taps into something deeply American: it was the force behind McCarthyism and anticommunism in the 1950s, and the Christian Right from the 1980s into our own day.

A lazy kind of journalism says that fascism appeals particularly to people who feel left behind: the embittered white working class, imperiled small business, rural America. This view ignores, historically, the fact that ardent followers of Hitler could be found in the urban bourgeoisie and that his strongest opponents were workers who had a tough time before the regime came to power. Forty years ago, when Jonathan Cobb and I studied white working-class families in America for our book *The Hidden Injuries of Class*, we did find racist attitudes among our subjects—and also nonracist ones. Some racists then were doing well, some nonracists felt left behind. And this is equally true today: lots of workers throughout the country voted against Trump.

What, if anything, can be done about the regime now ruling America? The greatest threat to rule by misrule is policy that stands apart from the ruler's person. He wants policy to be an emanation of his desire, his will, his character. It's for this reason that the soft fascist has no real respect for law, because it regulates and standardizes impersonally. Just as Senator McCarthy fell hard when he could no longer rely on personalizing and demonizing, so Trump may fall soon—as I fervently hope he does. It will not be a knight in shining armor who comes to the rescue, but simply—as in the Russian enquiry—that he is at last held accountable by the rules.

SCHOOL OF TRUMP

PEDRO NOGUERA

Since Trump's inauguration in January, education policy has not been a priority for the new administration. And, given his views on the matter, including an obsession with promoting alternatives to "government schools," leaving it on the back burner may truly be a good thing.

After nearly a year in office, it's clear that other issues are more important to Trump: war (and threats of war), the economy, immigration (and the wall), hurricanes in Houston and Florida (and ignoring them in Puerto Rico), investigations into Russian hacking of the 2016 election, and, of course, health care. All of these have consumed so much of the president's time and attention that there's been little space left for questions of reading, writing, and arithmetic.

For those who fear what the Trump administration might do to remake education, after he called for expanding vouchers during his campaign and continued his long history of attacking teachers' unions, neglect might be the least bad option. Signs that education would be a low priority became clear when the administration announced its budget priorities in May and stated its desire to cut $9.25 billion (13.5 percent) from the U.S. Department of Education (DoEd). Trump's appointment of Betsy DeVos, a billionaire religious conservative from Michigan, set off many concerns, both because of her track record in expanding privately financed charter schools and because she is so clearly unqualified to lead the DoEd. However, with few resources at her disposal, she has not yet been able to do much to drive the department in a direction consistent with her conservative Christian values.

Of course, this doesn't mean she isn't trying, nor should we conclude that the Department of Education has been completely dormant. There is a reason why DeVos faces protests at many public appearances and now receives special protection from the U.S. Marshals Service at an average cost of over $500,000 a month.

DeVos has used her bully pulpit to promote school choice, the conservative panacea for all that ails American education, even when the subject isn't relevant to the audience she's been invited to address. At an appearance at historically black Bethune-Cookman University, where many of the students turned their backs on her, she went so far as to assert that historically black colleges and universities were "real pioneers when it comes to school choice"—an odd claim given that these institutions were founded due to the absence of choice: blacks were barred from attending white colleges.

Such misstatements are of course less consequential than the actions she would like to take and, in some instances, has already taken. Though Republicans criticized the Obama administration (and to some degree the Bush administration) for infringing on states' rights through policies such as No Child Left Behind and Race to the Top, under DeVos the DoEd has tried to have it both ways: claiming it wants to reduce the role of the federal government in mandating education policy to the states while also attempting to use ESSA (Every Student Succeeds Act) to scrutinize state policies related to standards and accountability. Conservatives have reacted with shock and surprise to these efforts.

According to Mike Petrilli from the conservative Fordham Institute, writing about criticism of Delaware standards under ESSA, "It is mind-boggling that the department could decide that it's going to challenge [the states] on what's ambitious."

The DoEd, like numerous other departments in the Trump administration, has yet to fill many key posts. But those appointments that have gone through have raised eyebrows and ire in some quarters. DeVos appointed Candice Jackson, who opposes affirmative action, to lead the Office for Civil Rights. More recently, on September 2, DeVos announced that she would appoint former DeVry University dean Julian Schmoke (DeVry is a private, for-profit college with only slightly more credibility than Trump University) to serve as head of the unit charged with investigating fraudulent loans. The fact that DeVry was required to pay a fine of $100 million in 2011 for issuing questionable loans was apparently not a disqualifier.

Other actions by Trump's DoEd have been suspect but barely newsworthy:

1. It reinstated hefty collection fees for some borrowers who have defaulted on federal loans.
2. DeVos tapped the chief executive of a private student-loan company to run the federal government's trillion-dollar financial aid operations.
3. She also backed the administration's decision to cease protecting the rights of transgender students and directed the Office for Civil Rights to consider transgender students' discrimination complaints on a case-by-case basis.

It is important to note that the department took quick action to implement a bipartisan initiative to help low- and moderate-income college students get year-round access to Pell Grants after

Congress approved the measure. However, in keeping with their war on science, the Republican-controlled House of Representatives considered (though did not bring to vote) the Rooney Amendment to the Make America Secure and Prosperous Appropriations Act, 2018 (H.R. 3354), which would have slashed federal funding for the nonpartisan Institute of Education Sciences (IES) by one-third, undermining the agency's mission of advancing independent scientific research and analysis.

As important as these issues are, since the election of Donald Trump, the biggest day-to-day challenges for educators are not so much the policies that have been adopted by the DoEd but rather the statements and actions of the president himself. Perhaps the most significant of these was the recent decision to eliminate DACA, an executive action that will turn 800,000 young people who were raised in the United States into fugitives unless Congress steps in to find a way to extend the protections ordered by Obama. Despite the fact that DACA has been supported by a broad array of business and religious leaders, many of whom were prominent Trump backers, the president has once again prioritized appeasing his largely white-nationalist base, which can't seem to get enough of his anti-immigrant policies and rhetoric.

Beyond DACA, the president's rhetoric and actions have raised a number of difficult questions for educators: How do teachers who call upon their students to respect one another explain the president's actions when he calls on followers to throw out hecklers at his rallies or belittles his opponents on Twitter? How does an educator who seeks to avoid politicizing the classroom speak fairly and objectively about the president when he is caught, repeatedly, telling obvious lies and making unsubstantiated assertions? Educators teach students to support their assertions with logic and scientific evidence. How does one explain a president who denies the existence of climate change?

How would a thoughtful educator who has admonished students not to bully or demean others say that it's still not acceptable, even when the president of the United States engages in schoolyard taunts ("Little Marco," "Lying Ted," and "Crooked Hillary")? How does a teacher explain Trump's frequent degrading and targeting of vulnerable groups (including Muslims, Mexicans, and the transgendered), his vilifying of journalists as "enemies of the people," and his equivocation when called upon to condemn Nazi and white-supremacist supporters? What does an educator who would prefer to avoid politics altogether do when nearly every day Trump uses language that is inflammatory, dangerous, and even bizarre? His actions and statements can't be ignored or even dismissed as a joke because, like it or not, he is the president of the United States and his actions and words have real consequences.

Despite their weight, at times it seems as though Trump's outrageous statements are an intentional distraction, a smoke screen intended to keep us from paying attention to the more dangerous and far-reaching actions of his administration. Who is paying attention when the Environmental Protection Agency attempts to roll back the Clean Water Act, when the Energy Department expands subsidies to the coal industry while eliminating those that were used to incentivize the use of wind and solar energy, or when the Justice Department reverses an order barring local police departments from obtaining and using military weapons and equipment? These actions will have a major long-term impact on our future, but they are considered far less newsworthy than the latest crazy tweet issued by the president at five a.m.

We are all receiving an education in politics and civics under Trump. Since his election, the number of recorded hate crimes has soared, and many of these incidents have occurred in schools. Mimicking the commander in chief, some children feel it's all right to chant "build the wall" when competing against Latino children, to call Muslim students terrorists or spray-paint swastikas on their lockers, or to target Jewish, black, Asian American, or gay classmates for bullying and mistreatment.

While Trump may not be impeached, his administration won't last forever. There will undoubtedly come a time in the not too distant future when we look back and ask ourselves how we allowed this to happen. Already, some educators blame themselves. Perhaps if we had done a better job teaching students how to distinguish between fake and real news, if we had promoted critical thinking rather than a regurgitation of facts and information, if we had actively encouraged rigorous debate based on evidence and well-reasoned assertions, maybe Americans would have been less easily manipulated and behaved as more intelligent voters. Most of all, had we studied U.S. history without the goal of promoting patriotism but with a willingness to confront ugly truths, maybe we would be less inclined to hold onto myths, lies, and distortions that have been passed down over generations.

The challenge for us now as we attempt to make it through the next three years of a Trump presidency is not merely to figure out how best to resist the dangerous, heartless, and reactionary moves of the administration but also to offer reasonable alternatives. In the field of education, that must begin with a renewed willingness to embrace critical thinking and scientific inquiry, and an emphasis on tolerance and empathy based on recognition of our interconnectedness, interdependence, and common humanity. Ultimately, it is by practicing and reinforcing values such as these that it will be possible for America to survive and recover after Trump.

TRUMP ON TWITTER

How a Medium Designed for Democracy
Became an Authoritarian's Mouthpiece

FRED TURNER

O n its face, Twitter appears to be a quintessentially democratic
medium. It promotes individualized expression, helps build
social networks, and, until recently, seemed to epitomize the
decentralized, highly individualized public sphere long called for
by liberal theorists and digital utopians alike. During Donald
Trump's campaign for president, however, it became an engine of
authoritarianism. Day after day, Trump spit out bits of fiction and
hyperbole. They piled up like tiny bricks, slowly but surely
walling off the landscape of reality. In its place, Trump hung bill-
boards depicting his own imagined magnificence. The mass media
pointed to Trump's tweets, ridiculed their lies, lampooned their
tone—and spread them far and wide. Slowly but surely, Trump
succeeded in doing what every fledgling totalitarian must. He
made the world look chaotic and dangerous. And through Twitter, he put himself at the center of the storm.

But how did this happen? Only twenty years ago, many scholars and journalists agreed: the internet and the World Wide Web
were sure to bring about more democracy. Virtual communities
would be hubs of collaborative intimacy. Blogs would give the man
in the street a voice. The strangleholds of corporate media central-
ization and state censorship would finally be broken and a new,

benevolent era of free expression would emerge. Now those hopes have been well and truly dashed—not only by Donald Trump's use of Twitter but by the failures of the Egyptian spring, the revelations of Edward Snowden, and the Russians' hacking of America's elections. All of these events have challenged our faith that the technologies of free expression necessarily bring democracy in their wake.

During his campaign, however, Trump went a critical step further. He successfully fused two elements that Americans have long regarded as implacably opposed: the authoritarian's will to centralize power and the democrat's faith in decentralized communication. When Trump tweeted, he demonstrated that the faith of a generation of twentieth-century liberal theorists—as well as their digital descendants—was misplaced: decentralization does not necessarily increase democracy, in the public sphere or in the state. On the contrary, the technologies of decentralized communication can be coupled very tightly to the charismatic, personality-centered modes of authoritarianism long associated with mass media and mass society. More frightening still, Trump's tweets have demonstrated that the technologies of individualized expression may not always stand as bulwarks to totalitarian power. They can in fact be made *cornerstones* of such power.

World War II and the Roots of Social Media

If so, Trump has overturned the intellectual consensus that gave rise to our faith in social media in the first place. To see how, we need to return to the start of World War II. In the late 1930s, American intellectuals, politicians, and journalists marveled at the rise of fascism in Europe and particularly in Germany. Many had long thought of Germany as the birthplace of Beethoven and Goethe and so as the epicenter of European high culture. How, they wondered, had this most sophisticated of nations fallen under the sway of Adolf Hitler? Many worried, too, at the rise of fascism in America. The racism and anti-Semitism that characterized Nazi doctrine were widespread in the United States at the same time. In 1938, for instance, the Catholic demagogue Father Coughlin broadcast his venomous anti-Semitism to a weekly radio audience of 3,500,000. In 1939, the Amerikadeutscher Volksbund drew 22,000 American fascists to a rally at Madison Square Garden in New York. An enormous banner reading "Stop Jewish Domination of Christian America" looked down on the stage. Later that year, after Hitler had marched into Poland, hundreds of American fascists marched down East Eighty-Sixth Street in New York behind American flags and Nazi swastikas as large crowds looked on without protest.

To observers at the time, the question was, why?

Today, most historians would probably look for an answer in the economic chaos of the era. But at the time, many Americans pointed to the power of the mass media. They made two distinct though often overlapping cases. The first was primarily structural and made by American journalists and German refugee intellectuals such as Shepard Stone and Theodor Adorno. The second was primarily psychological and made by anthropologists and psychologists such as Margaret Mead and Gordon Allport. Both groups noted that the leaders of Germany and America had taken hold of large, centralized media systems. The structuralists believed that the one-to-many design of mass media technologies in and of themselves forced audiences to tune their senses toward a single, powerful source. When they did, these analysts argued, they became vulnerable to whatever charisma the source might possess. Moreover, simply by turning together in a single direction, audiences rehearsed the one-to-many structure of fascism. In the process, the structuralists suggested that they ceased to reason and became members of an unthinking mass.

Figures such as Mead and Allport feared this process, too. In 1940 they helped form the Committee for National Morale, a group of sixty scholars who aimed to advise President Roosevelt on the best ways to establish democratic unity. Members of the committee generally subscribed to the theories of Franz Boas and the culture and personality school of anthropology. That is, they believed that every society had a modal personality type. It was the role of the family to cultivate this type in their children and so help them to adjust to their culture. When children left the family, committee members believed that media tended to sustain the socialization process begun at home. Most of them agreed with the structuralists that mass media tended to produce an authoritarian personality style. They also associated that style with German culture and with fascism more generally. How, they asked, could Americans produce a mode of media that would cultivate a democratic form of personality? And what would such a personality type look like anyway?

Their answers to these questions laid the cultural groundwork for social media. A democratic person, they argued, would be a psychologically whole individual, able to freely choose what to believe, with whom to associate, and where to turn their attention. A democratic personality would embrace others and celebrate their differences while retaining their own sense of separateness. Members of the committee believed that insofar as mass media promoted undifferentiated experience, it also promoted an undifferentiated, mass society. They argued that if they were to defeat the Axis, media makers would have to develop a multisource medium for propaganda. Only among an *array* of images and sounds could Americans cultivate the diversity of views that might sustain both unity and individuality.

In 1942, the Bauhaus refugee Herbert Bayer and the American photographer Edward Steichen brought the committee's ideas to life in *Road to Victory*, a huge exhibition of pro-American images at New York's Museum of Modern Art. There they hung photographs above, below, and around museum goers with the aim of democratizing their perceptions. As they moved among the pictures, viewers were meant to choose the ones they found most individually meaningful but to do it together. If the structure of mass media modeled the one-to-many structure of fascist government, the many-to-many nature of the encounters promoted by *Road to Victory* modeled its egalitarian alternative.

Road to Victory was the first in a long line of such exhibitions that stretched across the Cold War. By the 1960s, these exhibitions had become models for the multimedia performances of the San Francisco counterculture. On the shores of California, audiences again surrounded themselves with media in order to liberate their minds. But now the critique of fascism and mass media had become something subtly different: a critique of bureaucracy and mass society. Before long, locals like Steve Jobs seized on this new critique and on the idea that decentralized media technologies could democratize their users' perceptions to promote computers as tools of democratic revolution. Today the founders of Bay-area social media firms from Facebook to Twitter make the same claims, though in a new idiom: Social media will allow us to present our authentic selves to one another, they say, to "connect," and so, by implication, form an egalitarian, even potentially antiauthoritarian solidarity.

Authoritarian Individualism

Trump's capture of the presidency has visibly betrayed the anti-authoritarian promise of digital media. It has also revealed a critical flaw in the thinking that underlies it. Since World War II, many Americans have imagined that totalitarian societies are by definition regimented, hyper-bureaucratized, hierarchical, and emotionally numb. The emblems of such societies are the gulag and the concentration camp. Particularly after the 1960s, we have tended to imagine free societies as just the opposite: unregimented, antibureaucratic, egalitarian, and suffused with feeling. The emblems of a free society today, at least on the left, are the open-air rock concert and the sit-in. We are free, we believe, when we speak our individual truths together.

Yet anyone who sat in the mud at Woodstock knows how far from utopia a rock concert can be. And anyone who has ever had successful surgery at a hospital will respect the value of hierarchy, bureaucracy and disinterested reason. The critique of mass society and mass media that so animated Americans during and after World War II has left us blind to the ways in which individualism itself can be summoned to serve authoritarian ends. The Committee for National Morale, for instance, saw authentic individuality and the interpersonal sphere of action as key sources of resistance to fascism. The commune builders of the 1960s did too. Today both the performance of individual authenticity and the interpersonal sphere have become weapons in Donald Trump's assault on the institutions of American democracy.

Consider the question of Donald Trump's character. During the election, Hillary Clinton harped on his tempestuous, bullying style, assuming that it would alienate voters. It didn't. To many voters, Trump's carefully cultivated ability to wear his feelings on his sleeve made him appear more authentically himself. Trump mastered the idiom of mediated authenticity on reality TV's *The Apprentice*. There he depicted himself not only as a masterful manager but as a man flung here and there by his anger, his drive, his affections. Today on Twitter he repeats the performance. Trump's Twitter stream alternates between self-congratulatory announcements of his achievements and bombastic attacks on those he sees as enemies. Sen. Charles Schumer is "Cryin' Chuck Schumer." Former FBI director James Comey is a "phony." And of course, the mainstream media are "Fake News."

Many see these outbursts as signs of a president who can't control his emotions and so of Trump's weakness. But to many of his supporters, they are signs of his just being himself. On Twitter, Trump's tempestuousness is a sign of his authenticity as a person. Displaying that authenticity is one of the ways he claims the right to our attention and, with it, our political support. The historical irony is almost overwhelming: Trump has taken the logic of individual authenticity that animated the New Left in 1968 and American liberalism for thirty years before that and put it to work as a new mode of authoritarian charisma. Thirty years ago, anti–Vietnam War protestors presented themselves to those in Washington as authentic individuals bent on challenging a state gone off the rails. Today, their place has been taken by Donald Trump.

To be clear, I'm not trying to equate Trump's name-calling with mass marches on the Capitol. What I'm trying to do is make visible the consequences of an intellectual logic left over from the fight against fascism. The performance of authentic individuality does not necessarily free us from authoritarianism. Nor does authoritarianism always stalk us in the gray uniforms of German troops. On the contrary, the performance of individuality can help make the case that a particular individual represents a set of political interests *in their bodies*. In the 1960s, the notion that the personal is political drove any number of social movements. But the notion of an embodied, personalized politics is also central to authoritarianism. In settings ranging from Franco's Spain to Putin's Russia, authoritarian leaders have claimed to uniquely manifest the "will of the people" in their facial expressions, the strength of the people in their own muscles, the anger of the people in their voices. In fact, they have often offered this ability to personalize the political as a justification for seizing power.

Trump has done the same thing on Twitter. In the twentieth century, mass-media theorists often believed that charismatic authoritarian leaders had to first bring the bodies or minds of their audiences together in one place before they could work their hypnotic magic. That place might be a Nuremberg-style rally, or a one-to-many, geographically dispersed radio listening experience. Today, however, when Trump tweets, he presents himself as if he were part of a conversation among friends. Part of that presentation is a function of the medium's structure. Individual tweets arrive on a feed that almost certainly contains a wide array of sources. Depending on how users configure their Twitter streams, those sources may very well include friends, family, and colleagues. Much as midcentury authoritarians could use radio to broadcast their voices into the intimacy of the family living room, so now Trump can use Twitter to insert himself into the company of a user's chosen conversation partners. Trump also works hard to suggest to that his intimate circle—and through Twitter, yours—includes the rich and powerful. "Great meeting with a wonderful woman today, former Secretary of State Condoleeza Rice!" he tweets.

Here Trump's performance of individual authenticity, his raw emotionalism, make perfect sense. Trump tweets like a teenaged girl—not just in frequency but in genre and diction. On July 25, 2016, for instance, he tweeted "I was @FoxNews and met Juan

Williams in passing. He asked if he could have pictures taken with me. I said fine. He then trashes on air!" The blend of name dropping ("Juan Williams") and the "He-wanted-to-be-with-me-but-then-he-dissed-me" framing is straight from the High School Mean Girl Power Play Handbook. In the mass-media era, few presidential candidates would have spoken in such a casual, petulant idiom, at least in public. To do so would have been to diminish their power. Like a midcentury authoritarian, Trump builds his claims to power on constructing the sense that he feels the pain of his audience. Yet he has reworked the rostrum-pounding style of the twentieth century dictator for a new media era. On Twitter, his petulance is par for the course. By showing it, he demonstrates that he is a human being like his readers and like the friends whose tweets surround his in their feeds. He is a person like them.

Except of course, he isn't. That's the tyrant's trick: to pretend to act on behalf of the people while leading them down a dark alley and robbing them blind. The trick is as old as time. And it was a trick that twentieth-century scholars, journalists, and media makers hoped to prevent by breaking up one-to-many media and replacing them with multisource media surrounds. As he speaks on Twitter, a descendant of those surrounds, Trump undermines the assumptions at the heart of their work. Authoritarian charisma is not medium-dependent. Nor are authentic individuality, the intimate social sphere, or flexible, collaborative networks necessarily enemies of totalitarianism. Today, it is only key institutions—the courts, the press, and even the FBI—who stand in the way of Trump's becoming a charismatic autocrat in the mold of Vladimir Putin. These bulwarks remind us that in an era of authoritarian individualism, what democracy needs first and foremost is not more personalized modes of mediated expression. It is a renewed engagement with the rule of law and with the institutions that embody it.

NOTE

This essay was adapted from the author's essay in Pablo J. Boczkowski and Zizi Papacharissi, eds., *Trump and the Media* (Cambridge, MA: MIT Press, 2018). Revised June 4, 2018.

TRUMP'S ATTACK ON KNOWLEDGE

CRAIG CALHOUN

On any particular policy, we can always hope President Trump will flip-flop. Expel the Dreamers; save the Dreamers. Maybe he'll keep the United States in the Paris climate accords after all. Threaten Kim Jong-un but not really blow up the world. One thing we can know for sure: whatever Trump does, it won't be on the basis of knowledge—not even, it would appear, knowledge of his own enduring values.

Trump is resolutely against knowledge. It's not just that he doesn't have much or that too much of what he thinks is true is really false. The very idea of knowledge seems to make him uncomfortable. He takes the notion that he can't make up whatever truth he wants as a personal affront, a limit to his autonomy, and an insult to his narcissistic ego. He believes in being smart—and brags frequently about his IQ. I'm sure he believes in information, preferably insider information about stock trades, real-estate opportunities, or what his enemies are up to. He just doesn't believe in knowledge.

Correct information is a first step in knowledge. But whether it is embodied in theories or practical reason, knowledge is more than just discrete and isolated facts. It is the ability to judge alleged statements of fact, the ability to put these together in meaningful ways—to "connect the dots" and to understand the implications.

We know Trump is at ease with lying. He lies habitually, lies to himself, and believes his lies. His claim that more people attended his inauguration than Obama's could be checked and proven false by photos, videos, and Park Service reports—but that didn't seem to bother him (though contradiction on that basis did). He lied to get elected. He lied about his failure to marshal assistance for Puerto Rico after Hurricane Maria. He lies about economic policy and about the risks of nuclear war. He lies about health care and the environment. He lies about whether Mexico is really going to pay for a wall on our mutual border. He lies about his own behavior. This is pervasive and extraordinarily damaging. But lying is not the whole issue.

Ignorance as Well as Deceit

Trump mocks experts and panders to poorly supported opinions. He favors ad hoc policy making over careful analysis and preparation. If Donald Trump baked, he would yell at cakes to rise instead of looking at a recipe.

Trump's contempt for knowledge shapes his approach to appointing government officials, the gathering of official data, funding education and science, and relating to the news media. It extends to contempt for citizens' right to know what their government is doing and for the government's need for knowledge to do its work. This amounts to an attack that threatens to undermine both good governance and one of the foundations of democracy.

Climate change is a prime example. Trump ignores scientific findings about the causes of climate change, encourages public misunderstanding, and makes policy decisions at odds with what science shows. He seems to do this for short-term political expediency, not because of any deep-seated disagreement with prevailing science. It is not that he weighs arguments and evidence pro and con and simply reaches nonstandard conclusions. He shows no willingness to be guided by scientific knowledge—including economic and social-science analyses of mitigating and adapting to climate change. When he asserts that he can bring back coal, he wins cheers from workers desperate for jobs, but he misleads them about their real prospects—not least because coal has declined for economic as well as ecological reasons.

Or again, Trump maligned several of his immediate predecessors when he asserted falsely that previous presidents never called the families of soldiers killed in combat. But this doesn't seem to have been an intentional lie, just a rush to build himself up at the expense of his predecessors with no regard for the truth.

Trump hurries to speak—or tweet—without first finding out what is true. He is like a comedian who tests a joke by seeing whether audiences laugh. If his lines win cheers from crowds, then they are true enough to repeat. But those cheers are not tests of knowledge, only of popularity among self-selected followers. The confusion is ominous.

Blocking Knowledge the Government Needs

Trump's contempt for truth and honesty is manifest in the many lies he told during his campaign and continues to tell as president. But Trump's attack on knowledge is more than merely mendacity.

Someone could respect knowledge a great deal and lie simply to deprive others of it.

Trump avoids knowledge. He makes policy watching Fox News at three a.m. rather than on careful analyses of evidence and arguments. He accepts reports from his aides that cite no data, evidence, or sources but merely summarize opinions. He disdains the work of intelligence agencies and analysts. He makes no effort to build an administration that brings expertise and honest evidence to its handling of major issues. These all reveal a remarkable conviction that his uninformed opinions are better than actual knowledge. This is the hubris.

Trump has left the presidential Council of Scientific Advisors empty. Indeed, he has so little respect for scientific knowledge that he didn't invite America's Nobel Prize winners to the White House. He's ignored the White House Office of Science and Technology Policy, failing to appoint a director. He has cut funding to the U.S. Census, a primary source of honest information about what's happening in America, linked to the effective administration of a wide range of U.S. government programs and even the establishment of fair electoral districts. In the name of reducing regulation, he backs efforts to limit research and data collection to identify risks and inform policy on issues from pharmaceuticals and health care to toxic chemicals in the environment.

Along with congressional Republicans, Trump attempted to repeal the Affordable Care Act without making clear what would be put in its place. This reflects not only a cavalier attitude to the well-being of citizens but a disregard for the importance of knowledge—in government and in public efforts to monitor government. The Congressional Budget Office is a nonpartisan agency mandated by law to supply accurate knowledge about the implications of legislation. It revealed that 22 million more Americans would be uninsured if the repeal bill passed. In response,

Trump and some Republican congressional leaders proposed to slash the CBO's budget or even abolish it.

Trump makes much of being a businessman, but he seems to think business is centrally a matter of bluffing, bargaining, and bullying. In fact, business is based in significant part on knowledge—of how production processes work, of what clients or customers want and what suppliers can provide, of how to recruit and retain employees. Innovation doesn't just happen; it is based on knowledge. Markets depend on the availability of accurate business information. Regulation ensures honest disclosure rather than secrecy or deceit. Businesses are expected to have sound financial accounts and auditors who know how to evaluate them. And this becomes more important the larger and more complex the businesses and the markets.

Knowledge is similarly required to rebuild the country's infrastructure, to organize health care and education, to regulate the banking system, and to set economic or trade policy, environmental policy, and telecommunications and IT policy. Government is required—and requires knowledge that can be taught and checked—because all of these involve complex and very large-scale processes, not just interpersonal transactions that can be managed by two or three people face-to-face based on unsystematic learning from personal experience and anecdote.

This is why education is so important—and the Trump administration attack on public schools so disastrous. Just as dangerous are the proposals Trump endorses to tax graduate students when universities waive their tuition fees.

Knowledge is not all "book learning." It is also embodied in practical skills—like cooking, making a plumbing system work, or filing a tax return correctly. But in a complex society—and a complex structure of global relationships—it is vital to complement the knowledge gained from experience and embedded in practical expertise with the capacity to use data and conduct analyses to grasp how things work on larger scales.

Knowledge is needed throughout government. Wherever complex processes are at stake and wherever it is crucial to understand what others may do, then knowledge is necessary. The military knows that knowledge is crucial. Generals don't organize troop movements just on hunches—or shouldn't. They investigate conditions and constraints; they gather intelligence on enemy actions; they model possible consequences. We would think it outrageous if the Pentagon just guessed at whether it could move enough supplies to a field of battle to support the soldiers it sends there—and when Pentagon logistics fail, there is harsh criticism.

In general, the U.S. military operates with a high level of knowledge and invests heavily in continually improving its knowledge base. The rest of the government should do the same. But Trump has presided over not only budget cuts but also a widespread hollowing out of those government agencies that should be sources of knowledge.

The State Department is a glaring example. Evidently Trump does not think U.S. relations with other countries or participation in organizations like the International Monetary Fund should be based on knowledge. He and his secretary of state have left empty many of the positions required to understand foreign countries, what they might do, and how U.S. actions will be perceived and with what consequences. Trump tries to substitute bluster and bluff for knowledge in dealing with North Korea and China. He does not make a serious effort to know what is going on. He watches Fox News and he guesses. Indeed, he has failed to appoint ambassadors to a quarter of the world's countries. Jobs for intelligence and policy analysts also sit vacant. He treats intelligence agencies with contempt.

This is not an America-first, pro-sovereignty policy. It is incompetence. But it is also resistance to gaining and using knowledge. It affects not just diplomacy in general but key areas like cybersecurity, nuclear weapons, and policies on trade and tariffs.

Trump has appointed people to senior positions—like White House press secretary—who are laughably (and frighteningly) out of their depth. Other members of the Trump administration are smart enough but bring little knowledge of the fields in which they are called to work or the agencies they are charged with administering. Some are simply advocates for industries with a financial interest in policy rather than committed to using all available knowledge to design the best policy for the country. This may be because Trump doesn't like whole areas of policy. He's happy to have an incompetent head of the EPA because he doesn't want the EPA to make or administer good environmental policy. He'd like to close it or have it be ineffective.

But Trump also appoints intelligent officials who do seem to know what they are doing, including former generals and corporate CEOs. Presumably he does want to have successful policies in some areas. But it is not clear he gives much respect to the genuine knowledge of his own appointees. He demands absurd displays of flattery from his cabinet. He announces and sometimes denounces policy on the spur of the moment, without even telling the relevant cabinet secretary, let alone conferring on the decision. He undercuts their efforts—as when he told Secretary of State Tillerson he was "wasting his time" on North Korea. Trump's contempt for knowledge undermines the work of those who do bring expertise to their jobs. Perhaps this signals a fear that their knowledge will diminish his authority or be used to challenge his personal opinions.

The Authority of Knowledge

Believing in knowledge means accepting that it commands authority. While there may be no accounting for taste, as the saying goes, there is accounting for knowledge. It is shared among different people on the basis of reasons to believe, of modes of validation including, most crucially, logic and evidence. Whether one prefers Mexican food to Chinese or opera to jazz may be merely a matter of taste, but there are right and wrong answers to questions like which country is larger—or which has the greater trade imbalance with the United States.

Where questions are more complex, science is crucial. Science is a method for producing knowledge, checking it, and improving it, notably by experiment and other sources of empirical evidence and by theory and other applications of logical reasoning. Scientific knowledge is also the basis of less systematic but powerful real-world testing: it produces applications that work; it makes sense of what we do and technologies we use every day. Electricity really does power my toaster. Airplanes heavier than air really do fly.

Alas, I don't know very much about aerodynamics. My trust in the science that underpins the design and manufacture of engines and wings and the training of pilots is partly based on experience—not falling out of the sky. But it is also based on respect for expertise: the knowledge that enables engineers to make good designs, companies to build good manufacturing facilities, and pilots to make good decisions in the air. I could try to check up on each of these, but without becoming an expert myself that would be hard, and no one could become an expert in every area of knowledge.

This is one of the main reasons we benefit from government agencies—and insurance companies and courts—that do this checking for us. And this is why it is so dangerous that Trump wants the government to rely less on knowledge. Neither he nor anyone else knows everything there is to know on every topic.

Similarly, lawyers are expected to know what is required to make a contract sound, not rely on ad hoc formulations. When the law is unclear, courts exist to resolve disputes. Judges exercise judgment, but based on knowledge of the law, not simply on their personal preferences. As in the case of science, the authority of knowledge rests in part on the ability to check what is argued, for example, to appeal a case to a higher court.

To make knowledge open to checking, challenge, and reconsideration, it ideally should be public. This is especially important in a democracy, where one of the key rights of citizens, one of the central ways in which they may be said to have power, is to reexamine government decisions on the basis of the same knowledge available to legislators. One of the important roles of regulatory agencies is to make sure adequate information is available for this—for, say, consumer protection. But even where knowledge is necessarily restricted—by privacy concerns or security classification, for example—it is important that it be subject to scrutiny and correction by competent specialists. Inside the CIA and other U.S. government agencies there are capacities for such review—though they are now threatened when their findings are politically unpopular.

A Crisis of Trust

The authority of knowledge was in crisis before Trump. He is symptom as well as dramatic exacerbation of that crisis. He was elected partly because a significant number of U.S. citizens distrusted the experts and institutions that are meant to be sources of knowledge. They found truth not so much in detailed policy analyses as in shouts that the "elites" can't be trusted.

Trump campaigned against knowledge. He systematically discourages relying on knowledge. He publicly devalues it, mocks it in tweets, belittles those who raise evidence-based questions about his policy preferences. This worked for him in connecting to the large part of the American public that had become disillusioned with experts and elites.

Perhaps a third of the electorate seems willing to give credence to whatever Trump says—and refuses to take seriously those who contradict him. These millions of people are not just independent, self-mobilizing anti-intellectuals. Nor did their resentment of elites simply grow spontaneously. They have been guided and goaded by organized and well-funded efforts to persuade them not to trust established institutions and experts and to have faith in alternative narratives and news sources. These efforts work as well as they do because they are reinforced by the polarization of American public discourse and the containment of different accounts in different echo chambers. At least for some, evidence doesn't really matter, facts are whatever a website you like says they are, and a politician understood to be on the "right side" can get away with saying anything.

Social media are not friends to in-depth inquiry, rational-critical discourse, or reliance on knowledge. They do expand communication, and of course they are used to circulate serious analyses as well as jejune commentary, cat pictures, and Russian propaganda and disinformation. But vulnerability to hacking and intentional circulation of fake news are major issues. So are business models and reliance on algorithms that discourage effective editing of the posts on Facebook, Twitter, and the others. But social media didn't create the political polarization that they now exacerbate.

It is not just the political Right that has segmented itself into a separate discursive arena; the Left has, too. Together they have drastically weakened the political center. Instead of a public sphere where views are subjected to debate and rational-critical analysis—ideally informed by knowledge—we seem currently to have only counter-publics, separate arenas trying to achieve their own critical mass and contest the alleged domination of a nonexistent conventional wisdom.

It doesn't help that necessary expertise is embedded in a structure of unnecessary inequality. This complicates making an effective argument for knowledge. The best-educated experts have attended schools and enjoyed careers that lead them to be not only part of a knowledge elite but also participants in a wider elite culture. This involves not just ostensibly refined tastes but also the idea that the hierarchy of tastes clearly reflects underlying value. Too many embrace an ideology of meritocracy that pretends unequal outcomes are the result of differences in talent and effort, ignoring the impact of very unequally distributed opportunities.

And along with other kinds of inequality, differences in educational opportunities have grown more extreme in recent decades. Knowledge has come to be treated as a private good to be bought, directly or indirectly, rather than a public good to be shared democratically. Parents, for example, focus on getting their kids into the Ivy League to the exclusion of making sure public universities offer a strong alternative available to all; even public universities have been drawn into constant pursuit of hierarchical distinction. When elites begin to see their own educational and occupational success as evidence that they are better than others, giving them the illusion that privilege is really meritocracy, they are apt to add insult to injury, helping to provoke just the sort of crisis we are seeing.

Elite management of American and global affairs has not been an unmitigated success. Knowledgeable elites with degrees from good universities presided over growing inequality, massive financial crisis, decline of American hegemony, and an escalating national debt held largely by China. Elites may have been in the foreground of calling for action on climate change, but they have also tolerated policies producing it. Elites made Middle Eastern policies that brought thousands of deaths—mainly of nonelites— and greater terrorist threats in the course of a depressing and long-lasting military engagement. Trust declined in part because elites were not altogether trustworthy.

Other factors undermined the authority of knowledge even before Trump. Academic attacks on problematic "master narratives" sometimes turned into generalized debunking and challenges to the very ideas of truth and even truthfulness. A false choice between excessive certainty and relativism obscured genuine capacities to move from weaker to stronger knowledge. Ideologues exploited confusion about how science works to portray scientific theories as mere conjectures and imply that because science is a method for continual improvement there is no strong reason to trust current formulations. The Bush-era neoconservative denigration of a "reality-based community" too focused on facts instead of creating a new reality helped to usher in the appeal to "alternative facts" made famous by Trump aide Kellyanne Conway.

Media trivialization has also sometimes undermined trust in scientific knowledge. Hardly a day goes by without newspaper and TV reports of allegedly scientific diet and health "news." This constantly shifting advice, often based on taking single studies out of context rather than connecting different dimensions of knowledge, encourages the view that what science proclaims today may be dismissed tomorrow. And it doesn't take a lot of probing to realize that the constant news reports reflect not just a relatively mindless side of the media but also the organization of medical research in a constant pursuit of publicity and funding.

Quite outside the Trump administration and the government, contemporary America faces an erosion of public access to knowledge and openness to scientific assessment and error correction. Increasingly, the data needed for scientific research, checking up on both government and business, and even managing our personal affairs is either not freely available or privately controlled by business corporations. As a result, data quality is often not checked. Access is restricted. And security breaches expose ordinary citizens to extraordinary risks.

The Challenge

A preference for Donald Trump's bombast and populist gestures is a horribly counterproductive response to genuinely problematic policies and elites too complacent to rethink them adequately. But it does point to a chronic challenge for modern, complex societies. The systems on which they depend—technological, governmental, economic, organizational, media—can only be run on the basis of significant specialized knowledge. This makes expertise critically important. Yet it also creates the potential that experts will pursue their self-interests alongside national (or global) interests and that they will be insufficiently attentive to the implications of their policy choices for a variety of fellow citizens different from themselves.

The fact of this challenge doesn't excuse the racism and other repugnant attitudes commonly bundled into populist resentments. But it does help us see one of the ways in which societies dependent on advanced knowledge become vulnerable to attacks on knowledge. That knowledge is necessary doesn't guarantee that it will be used well, shared widely, or kept distinct from claims to status or power.

It's hard for me to accept that the president of the United States doesn't like knowledge. I grew up in a household where knowledge was an unchallenged value. My parents read the newspaper and watched the *Huntley-Brinkley Report*. They asked how I did in school. They read the Bible. They bought my brother and me the *World Book Encyclopedia* (from a salesman who said it would help us do better in school and even reach beyond what the schools offered in our small Kentucky town). Aiming higher, they even bought a set of gold-embossed leather Great Books endorsed by the University of Chicago, together with its own bookcase, to stand in our front hall as evidence of the fact that we were the sort of people who believed in knowledge. They were not alone. They were part of a broad middle that has all but vanished with political polarization and economic inequality.

Like many, I find Trump shocking and offensive. He is crude. He makes immoral policies. But his attack on knowledge may do damage that far outlasts his repugnant, embarrassing presence in the White House.

What is at stake is not just that Trump makes decisions in ignorance or that as a result he leads the U.S. government in extremely risky ways. That's bad enough; indeed, it's terrifying. But what's ultimately at stake is the authority of knowledge itself, for Trump is leading an effort to make knowledge less available, less trusted, and less used throughout society.

Yet choices and, thus, freedom depend on knowledge as well as values. If you have no idea of the consequences of your actions, you cannot make good choices. Unintended consequences will potentially overwhelm you and thwart what seemed good intentions.

And if the government fails to institutionalize support for knowledge and reliance on knowledge, both democracy and good governance will suffer. This is the dark road Trump and Trumpism are taking us down.

PART II

The Collapse

How We Got Here

THE DEVASTATED HOUSE OF LABOR

MARGARET LEVI

American workers are heterogeneous politically as well as racially, ethnically, and educationally. Unions are equally mixed. Some unions focus primarily on the narrow economic interests of their members, and others have strong commitments to social justice. Despite their differences, virtually all unions and their confederations in the post-WWII era increasingly advocated racial inclusiveness and greater economic equality. The unions, while often protectionist on trade, used their members' electoral clout and their organizations' money on behalf of social safeguards and public goods. But the once-strong house of labor—a significant force in American politics and economics since at least the 1930s—has been largely devastated.

Union decline has been long in coming and is now close to complete, and Trump is among the beneficiaries politically. Without empowered labor unions—or something that takes their place—it is far harder to wage an effective fight against Trump and for a more equitable distribution of power and profits. Unions lobby to protect and expand rights, incomes, pensions, education, health care. They offer civic education and mobilize voters and voices. As they shrink in scope, fewer people benefit from their negotiating strength, and more workers from once heavily unionized regions of the country veer rightward.

Let us be clear. Progressivism is not a necessary trait of workers, even among those most harmed by the excesses of capitalism, by exploitative employers, or by opportunistic politicians. Friedrich Engels was mistaken in his prediction that the working class would succeed in using "paper stones"—that is, the ballot—to vote in a socialist alternative to capitalism. He failed to comprehend either the numerical growth of the middle class, which historically has had little interest in creating a socialist system, or the disinterest in socialism exhibited over the last century-plus by so much of the working class in the advanced capitalist democracies.[1]

This disinterest has become particularly clear in recent decades in the United States, as symbolized by the rise of so-called Reagan Democrats, blue-collar workers who cast their lot with Reagan's Republicans. Union members often value and attempt to protect jobs in industries that harm the environment and climate, and they are also far too often opponents of liberal immigration policies. Reagan played on this, and, a generation on, Trump has done so even more.

What happened? After all, American unions were once a key component of a larger social movement and a bulwark of the Democratic Party from the New Deal years on.[2] In the nineteenth century, the Knights of Labor aimed to build a class-based coalition for change. The Seattle General Strike of 1919 remains a beacon of the potential for normal workers to democratically govern a city on behalf of all.[3] The great strikes of the 1930s were generally waged by industrial unions committed to social-democratic and sometimes communist principles, to the point that corporate and governmental leaders feared a Bolshevik revolution in the United States.

The key to progressive labor organizations is having leaders and governance structures that provide credible information about how the world really works, as well as education about issues that are crucial to their members' and potential members' economic and social well-being.[4] Some unions actively encourage their members to make collective commitments to causes that are far beyond what they can demand of employers in terms of material gains. Most have (or had) leaders immersed in syndicalist, socialist, or communist ideology, and at least some of their grassroots members adhered to similarly radical political values. Many truly adhered to the old Wobbly and current ILWU (International Longshore and Warehouse Union) slogan: "An injury to one is an injury to all"—with the all being all exploited people, not just those in their union. The ILWU is an exemplar here: the union refused to ship scrap iron to Japan after its invasion of Manchuria in 1938 and later they refused to unload goods from Apartheid South Africa. Although the personal costs were potentially high (lost pay, jail, lost jobs), the union and its members persisted.

For the first few decades after World War II, they persisted in the face of growing institutional opposition. The 1947 Taft-Hartley Act facilitated firm-centered (rather than industry-wide) bargaining and in doing so made union organizing more difficult. Yet despite this, union power in America increased. So did the role of unions in popular culture: the meme was Big Labor as an equal with Big Business and Big Government. Major newspapers of the time regularly covered union actions. By the 1970s, more than 20 million Americans were in unions, which remained a vital part of the Democratic Party's coalition, helping to protect working people within the broader American economy.

Then things began to change—and union power began being rolled back, first gently and then with increasing ferocity. Several factors led to the devastation in the house of labor. Even in its heyday, the labor movement failed to represent that part of the labor force working in the agricultural, domestic, and low-end service sectors. After the Reagan onslaught, the employers regained the upper hand, knowing that government would either look the other way or actively assist in the employer campaign to undermine unions organizing more workers and effectively enforcing collective bargaining rights. Moreover, enough time had gone by since the acme of labor organizing that young workers no longer credited unions with the improvements in their standard of living. The combined loss of power and the increased focus of many unions on particularistic gains made it difficult for unions, even the large confederations, to block the policies that amplify inequality in the United States. One result in recent decades has been real wage declines even as U.S. productivity has grown.

At the turn into the twenty-first century, survey evidence reveals that workers still wanted unions.[5] A 2002 study, confirmed with additional data in 2005, found that more than 50 percent of nonunion, nonmanagerial workers preferred union representation. The percentages were particularly high among eighteen- to thirty-four-year-olds (58 percent), those with incomes under $40,000 (59 percent), and minorities (74 percent). Fifteen years on, it would be worth doing such an analysis today, particularly among younger workers. My own research on and experience with those employed in the new gig economy suggest that interest in having a voice no longer translates into interest in being represented by a union, an organization perceived as constraining individual prerogatives while taking a cut for doing so.

In 2016 the total union membership in the combined public and private sectors was only 10.7 percent of all nonagricultural wage and salary workers, or 14.6 million people.[6] Unions have always been weak in the South and in the noncoastal western states. For the industrial heartlands, the decline in membership over recent years is notable. South Carolina has the lowest membership at 1.6 percent. The highest southern state is Alabama, at 8.1 percent, placing it in a dead heat with Wisconsin, which used to be a union stronghold.

These aggregate figures hide the real story, however. Only 6.4 percent of private sector workers now belong to unions, down from the high of over 35 percent in 1954. By and large, what is keeping unions alive is government employment: 34.4 percent of public-sector workers belong to unions. And yet the future of public-sector unions is, arguably, tenuous.[7]

Note the reactions against them in once union-proud states such as Wisconsin. There is, in these states, growing antagonism among the public to the demands and strikes of government employees. At the same time, government austerity measures have further undermined the strength of the public sector. All evidence suggests that Trump will perpetuate the undermining of workers' rights and wages. He has yet to tweet much about government unions, but he froze employment in the civil service, chose a VP with a proven antiunion record, and appointed a union-hostile secretary of labor.

In 1947, the Taft-Hartley Act made it possible to create what became known as "right-to-work" laws, which enabled workers to opt out of dues paying even when gaining the benefits of representation. Eleven states, most of them in the South, immediately adopted "right to work" regulations. Another five more became "right to work" by 1955. Today twenty-eight states and Guam have this status. As a result, union power nationally has been decimated.

In the late 1990s and again in the Obama era, there was some guarded optimism that these trends could be reversed, that unions could regain some of their leverage, and that a new generation of labor activists might even take leadership on questions of equality and equity, both economic and racial.[8] There is no such hope with

Trump, a man with a long history of hostility to unions and to fair labor practices and whose interests lie in further decimating any source of potentially progressive opposition. He appeals to many workers but plays only to their basest interests and their current fears.

Without question, manufacturing—the basis of the grand industrial unions—has been disappearing from the United States for several decades. And whatever Trump's rhetoric around protectionism and manufacturing, it is most unlikely that he will be able to reindustrialize the heartlands. People are hurting, and they no longer believe that their children will be better off than they were. They are looking for a scapegoat, and they demand a silver bullet to restore what they once had. Instead of advocating for programs to assist those in need and those striving to prepare themselves for the transformation of the economy, Trump pushes his protectionist trade policies, a hard line on immigration, and tax reform, none of which will ultimately benefit those left behind by recent economic trends. He does this by making exaggerated and often decidedly false claims that American jobs have gone overseas or to new immigrants, and he ignores the role of technological change.

This strategy, while unlikely to actually generate manufacturing jobs in the United States, has the added benefit of demonizing unions—such as the National Domestic Workers Alliance and Service Employees International Union (SEIU)—that are growing in prominence and that disproportionately represent immigrant labor. Trump's analysis may be largely inaccurate, but it finds resonance among white workers, whose jobs are precarious and whose standard of living is falling. And it supports the efforts to weaken the labor movement further.

Some union members and former members *do* continue to engage in progressive social movements and strive to mobilize votes for politicians who will genuinely serve their interests. They are leading the way in campaigns to unionize low-income workers, to legislate the fifteen-dollar living wage, and to defend the Affordable Care Act. These campaigns deserve as much support and backing as we can provide.

But, according to the AFL-CIO, 3 percent more union members voted for Trump than voted for Romney, and 10 percent fewer for Clinton than for Obama.[9] Some of those union members—to our detriment and ultimately theirs as well—have turned to the angry and racist populism of the right. This sort of electoral upheaval has happened before: in Nazi Germany, in Fascist Italy, and in Peronist Argentina. However, in those cases, the unions themselves, not simply some of the union members, turned to the right. What we are seeing in America is different, representing a decline in organizational reach. Union activists may still be progressive, but their message of a wide-ranging cross-class coalition has lost its appeal to most of those in the labor force, as well as to many of their own members.

With the decline in unions, we lose a mediating association that has been critical to negotiating economic conflict and creating a countervailing balance to corporate power. It may be difficult, if not impossible, to revive the labor movement we once knew; the unions of the past are not the organizations that speak to the workers of today. With each transformation in the economy, a new form of unionism has arisen with its own particular strategies: craft unions controlled the supply of labor; industrial unions engaged in large-scale strikes; service unions rely on strikes but also class-action law suits and legislation.

We spend a lot of time worrying about candidates and proposed laws. The real challenge is to invent innovative mediating labor and other associations that meet the needs of citizens in the contemporary political economy. This means developing movements for mobilizing large numbers into cohesive wholes and inspiring adherents to act in the interest of others. Without such new and effective mediating associations, Trump will get a second term. Even worse, he will be but the first in the line of many autocratic presidents, tone-deaf to the workers and the poor, and indifferent to the rule of law and the norms of a civil society. And his successors are likely to be far more competent, effective, and destructive of what makes America great.

NOTES

1. Adam Przeworski and John Sprague, *Paper Stones: A History of Electoral Socialism* (Cambridge: Cambridge University Press, 1986).
2. J. David Greenstone, *Labor in American Politics* (New York: Vintage Books, 1969); Peter L. Francia, *The Future of Organized Labor in American Politics* (New York: Columbia University Press, 2006).
3. Victoria Johnson, *How Many Machine Guns Does It Take to Cook One Meal? The Seattle and San Francisco General Strikes* (Seattle: University of Washington Press, 2008); Jeremy Brecher, *Strike!* (Boston: South End Press, 1997).
4. John S. Ahlquist and Margaret Levi, *In the Interests of Others* (Princeton, NJ: Princeton University Press, 2013).
5. Richard Freeman, "Do Workers Still Want Unions? More than Ever!" Briefing Paper No. 182, Economic Policy Institute, February 22, 2007, http://www.gpn.org/bp182/bp182.pdf; Jake Rosenfeld, *What Unions No Longer Do* (Cambridge, MA: Harvard University Press, 2014).
6. "Union Membership (Annual) New Release," Bureau of Labor Statistics, January 26, 2017, https://www.bls.gov/news.release/union2.htm.
7. John S. Ahlquist, "Public Sector Unions Need the Private Sector (or Why the Wisconsin Protests Were Not Labor's Lazarus Moment)," *The Forum* 10, no. 1 (2012).
8. Bill Fletcher Jr. and Fernando Gapasin, *Solidarity Divided* (Berkeley: University of California Press, 2008); Dorian T. Warren, "'Labor in American Politics': Continuities, Changes, and Challenges for the Twenty-First-Century Labor Movement," *Polity* 42, no. 3 (2010): 286–92.
9. Sean Higgins, "Union Voters Swung Behind Trump, Richard Trumka Says," *Washington Examiner*, August 30, 2017, http://www.washington examiner.com/union-voters-swung-behind-trump-richard-trumka -says/article/2632984.

UNHOLY ALLIANCES

SHAMUS KHAN

Andrew Jackson had good reason to believe that his first presidential election, of 1824, had been rigged. He had won the popular vote but not an Electoral College majority. Jackson was hated by elite political players. The Tennessean's crass demeanor, uneducated manner, and disconnection from the dominant elite strongholds of Massachusetts and Virginia—all previous presidents had hailed from one place or the other—made him anathema to the gentry who had run the country since its founding a half century earlier. The House of Representatives denied Jackson the presidency and elevated John Quincy Adams instead, a man who, as the son of a former president and heir to an elite political legacy, represented just what Jackson was fighting against.

Four years later Jackson would reap his revenge, running a starkly populist campaign. He would mobilize twice as many voters as had ever gone to the polls in the brief history of the young republic, silencing the power of the elites with the voices of the people. Today we look back and view this popular mobilization as breaking the aristocratic elite's domination of American politics, shepherding in the first modern American president, and auguring a newly democratic sensibility in the rapidly growing country.

Jackson's ascension to power represented a fundamental challenge to the republic. Our political institutions were designed to be insulated from popular democracy. The Electoral College ensured that the president would not be directly elected. The Supreme Court has never been elected by the populace. Senators only began being directly elected after the passage of the Seventeenth Amendment, in 1913. American democracy had a core principle: keep the important parts away from the meddling influence of relatively unenlightened citizens. Let the competent elites do their job.

While Jackson's populism helped break elite control of democratic institutions, it was built, as most populisms are, on a narrowly circumscribed definition of "the people." Ethnic whites supported Jackson in no small part because of his ethnic cleansing of the nation. Commenting on the horrors unleashed against Native Americans by Jackson, Alexis de Tocqueville, who watched as the defeated tribal members were force-marched through Memphis, would write in his diary, "In the whole scene there was an air of ruin and destruction, something which betrayed a final and irrevocable adieu; one couldn't watch without feeling one's heart wrung. The Indians were tranquil, but sombre and taciturn. There was one who could speak English and of whom I asked why the Chactas were leaving their country. 'To be free,' he answered . . ."

Jackson's populism blended contempt for East Coast elites—those aloof, Enlightenment-era scholar-politicians whose worldview was shaped in colonial-era America—with a concerted effort to define and to limit who belonged in the United States: who held the keys to liberty and who, through racial and other exclusions, would have to leave our nation if they wanted to be free.

There is a core tension within our nation between the elitist structures of our institutions and the increasingly democratic sentiments of the country's culture. Sometimes, the democratic pull has resulted both in more participation and in more of an informed citizenry. At other times, however, it has slid into the exclusionary populism that Jackson embodied. Reformers have thus been obliged to navigate our politics between the Scylla of elite dominance and the Charybdis of populist exclusion.

Donald Trump's administration is a strange hybrid, somehow managing to crash our nation into this twin set of perils. On the one hand, Trump likes to fashion himself as a Jacksonian populist, a defender of white, male, red-blooded American-ness. On the other hand, his administration is peopled by plutocratic elites. It has proven to be a peculiarly ugly and incompetent combination. These titans of industry and billionaire "winners," few of whom have political experience, are the least competent and most corrupt group of political leaders that America has had in generations. And yet for much of Trump's base, animated more by a desire for the restoration of racial privilege than by a craving for competent governance, the failings are more than made up for by Trump's clear sympathies for white nationalism.

Some critics decry the Trump presidency as being "un-American." But in actuality it is part of a long political tradition, beginning before Jackson, that was fully embodied by the slave-owning founders of the country, who used the genteel language of liberalism and the Enlightenment to craft a political system based on racial slavery, gendered exclusions, and class hierarchies.

While ethnic exclusion is at the heart of Trumpian populism, it was not the only source of his appeal during the 2016 election. He also attacked a small cosmopolitan elite, exemplified, in his rhetoric, by Hillary Clinton and by out-of-touch mainstream journalists, who, he suggested, were more interested in looking across oceans than into their own land, seeing themselves as citizens of a global world rather than an American nation.

Trump appealed to the left-behind "real Americans"—those who feel they are the true inheritors of our nation and who believe that "outsiders" have been unfairly prioritized and pandered to in recent decades. The solution Trump sold them was to take back the nation and expel, imprison, or marginalize the others who benefited from a rotten alliance that threatened to change the exceptional ethno-cultural identity of this country.

While much as been written about the ethnic elements of Trump's appeal, less has been said about his cultural appeal. The intelligentsia's contempt toward him is based in no small part on his lack of "class" or, in more academic terms, "cultural capital." We revel in images of his coarseness—his tacky, gilded homes; the fact that he eats his steaks well-done and doused in ketchup; his loud, brash demeanor; the architectural disasters that are his branded buildings, to say nothing of his owning a gaudy casino. As the joke goes, Donald Trump is what poor people would do if they had money. But as Bourdieu helped us understand, money is but one part of the social organization of hierarchical relations. Trump revels in his boorishness, in his being culturally more in tune with "ordinary" Americans than with those elites who have but a fraction of his proclaimed wealth.

Ethnic whites, particularly men, are not wrong in thinking that they've lost their relative economic standing and their cultural dominance. In the last forty years, wages for women and minorities have markedly increased. Whites and men are still better off than almost all other groups, but the gap has closed considerably. In that same forty years, elites have almost completely captured the economic rewards of our increased productivity. They have increased their control of capital through stock ownership. The richest 300,000 Americans have seen their incomes increase almost 500 percent while the average American is stuck in place.

These two simultaneous processes—the elite seizure of economic growth and the relative advancement of women and nonwhites—provided a critical opportunity for a demagogue such as Trump. Seizing on the sentiment of relative deprivation, Trump suggested that a subgroup of elites had advantaged both themselves and an illegitimate set of Americans. This ruse capitalized on white men's sense that an unholy alliance of elites, women, and non-whites had taken the economic rewards and displaced white men from their traditional social, cultural, and economic pride of place.

Make no mistake: Trump's was not a working-class movement. Two-thirds of Trump voters made more than the median national income. Economic anxiety alone does little to explain the likelihood of a person voting for Trump. But throw into the mix racial and cultural animus, and you have a toxic electoral coalition that propelled him to the White House.

The Trump movement builds on an old form of populism, one that emphasizes those "left behind" by cultural and economic changes, focusing on the rights, position, and power of a specific group who are advantaged, but losing their relative position. This is a particular kind of democracy, where economic differences are bridged through ethno-cultural alliances. The rights of others, or of those who are not "the people," should be limited in order to maintain the dominance of that narrowly circumscribed group of "real Americans" who must be protected from the perils of a more tumultuous, more multiethnic and multilingual democracy.

Some, like Arlie Hochschild, have argued that the solution to our problems is to be more attentive to working-class white people and empathize more with their plight. Such an approach misguidedly puts a premium on "whiteness," asking nonwhites to compromise their struggles and pander to this wounded lion. Others, like Mark Lilla, suggest that solutions like Hochschild's would only represent a continuation of racial politics and argue that what we need to do is rekindle a more "colorblind" and universalist liberal tradition. Yet this approach ignores the racial and gendered bases of liberalism, where white men happily occupy the unmarked position—those without race or gender—and thereby are privileged in their capacity to suggest that their positions are not based in some "identity politics." Still others have suggested that what we need is to find a unifying umbrella under which to consolidate our movements; for many on the Left, that umbrella is "class." Yet class-based movements have often been predicated on exclusion and the dismissal of non-class-based concerns.

There are three lessons I draw from this meditation on "the big picture," one year after Trump's electoral win. The first is that we can't play a one-dimensional game in a multidimensional world. The idea that we can just singularly emphasize class or race or gender is as politically naive as it is ineffective. Trump was able to create cross-class alliances through critiques of elite culture; he was able, despite the allegations of sexual abuse and harassment against him, to use racial politics to mobilize a majority of white women to vote for him. Any political solution requires alliances across a wide range of dimensions—economic, religious, racial, gender, and culture—to be successful.

The second is that, if Trump has shown anything, it is that elites are not a monolith. Many among "the elite" clearly find his politics and policies, as well as his persona, distasteful, even grotesque. This opens up space for alliance building in opposition to the culture and the political movement that Trump is busy consolidating. There is currently no single American elite. Rather, there are competing elites, with different interests and bases of their social power. Political movements for durable change will require alliances with some of these elites. Mobilizing their resources—their ties to one another, their knowledge of institutions, their money, and their influence—will be crucial to the resistance. Elites will be necessary players in blocking Trump's excesses and minimizing the damage that his toxic racial and religious populism is unleashing on this complex, diverse, and geographically vast country.

Finally, inegalitarianism is a robust American political tradition. The present is not so much an aberration as a continuation of normal politics in America. Thus, as we look for effective routes of opposition we ought to consider leaning on organizing tools that have, in other chapters of the American story, worked to bend the arc of history in the direction of a more inclusive union.

We have long-established political traditions of dissent and of resistance. Black politics should be our guide, in no small part because of its association with the concept of "linked fate." How might we create cross-class, cross-culture, cross-gender alliances? The black political community's capacity to do this over a period of decades is perhaps unrivaled. This means spending less time thinking about how we can pander to the white vote and more time looking to black political communities for guidance in the politics of solidary across dimensions of difference.

Voters were right in sensing the building of an unholy alliance. But that alliance is not, as Trump suggested, between elite culture and a more diverse citizenry; it is, as Trump represents, between elite interests and white-nationalist sentiments. We must pivot elites away from the politics of interest and whites away from racial domination. A countermovement can appeal to both groups through morally grounded visions of equality and solidarity.

COALTHINK

GRETCHEN BAKKE

I f we trust the president, we believe that he is, if nothing else, a businessman. Towers glittering across real estates seem to proclaim the truth of this, but when it comes to coal, both business and sense exit the scene. Mercurial to his core, the diligence with which Mr. Trump maintains his fidelity to coal—the ferocity of his adoration of it—belies the notion that its use to him is that of simple political expediency. Symbolic of white working America, yes. Evocative of a 1950s, half-remembered and half-imagined, when environmental concerns impeded nothing, yes. But fuel of the future? This possibility hovers somewhere between unlikely and impossible.

The business case for the end of coal was well and solidly in place before Mr. Trump declared himself a candidate. Very few people have taken such a liking to the stuff as he has. Nobody really thinks that it will power the future, whether in America or elsewhere. Even China, which uses more coal than any other nation on earth, is making noises about moving on; even the chief executive of the American Coal Council admits that the industry has abandoned any plans to replace the retiring fleet of coal-burning power plants, once the backbone of American power. Even big money turns a blind eye toward coal. An executive at a venture-capital firm recently told me with a bit of a grin that nobody even knows what a coal plant is worth any more. It's possible that one should be paid for the purchase of such a plant, rather than the other way around.

The era of coal in the United States is over; some might say it is only "ending," but the fact that bygones will soon be bygones is not under serious debate. What is it then about coal that pleases the president so? The answer I think, is that it's the last solid thing. And this tangibility, this sense of there being a something to hold on to, has implications not just for the presidency but for the country's future.

Though I doubt that the president has actually ever touched coal, its solidity matters. It can be touched. It is there. Coal is a "known known" as Mr. Rumsfeld would have said, a stone one can grip in a fist. Whatever Mr. Trump's personal past with combustible ingots, I am more certain that he has never touched natural gas—all wisps and fumes. And I suspect he has never understood that the wind (deranging his hair) or the sun (contributing, perhaps, to his improbable tan) are harvestable despite being immaterial. He may well recognize the weather in its attempted disturbances of his daily rhythms, but he does not grasp the climate. The climate is not, strictly speaking, graspable. No hand can take it in. No man, no matter how tight his fist, can hold it to himself.

Climate, sunbeams, air, natural gas: they are more like ideas than objects. One must be capable and comfortable with abstraction to get them right. Let's add one more to the list, electricity. Who knows how it works, but at least when coal was the centerpiece of the electric-power system it was possible to imagine a material that grounded our remotely powered, information-dense world. Coal for power begat worlds of activity: mountains chopped down, pits excavated, veins followed, burrows made, workers straining backs, lungs straining black, train cars and rails moving combustible rocks to factories honorable in their complexity and reliability so long as the coal is there. Even the particulate nature of coal dust as a sort of midcentury pollution (like smog) is so much easier to imagine and deal with—even, in a strange, dysto-pian way, to romanticize—than are CO_2 and CH_4 and N_2O.

All of this digging, shipping, building, and combusting is the stuff of infrastructure: the means we use to build up a functional world that is, almost by its nature, substantive. That said, holding a material—a real hard tangible stone of a thing—is, at its core, the old way of infrastructure. Like the copper that goes into electric wires, the wood chopped up to build houses and make utility poles, the concrete poured into building foundations, it is a vis-ceral, necessary premise. These are reminders, perhaps, of the raw, industrial world that Mr. Trump was born into in the 1940s and certainly something that any real estate developer, any builder of things, can immediately understand and appreciate.

In a way, I like how Mr. Trump has pulled an awareness of materiality back into our modern world. As if to say, look beneath your feet: Whence that floor? That roadway? That runway? Look over your head: whence that ceiling, cabling, polystyrene? He gives us cause to remember that much of the work done is still done by men who sweat. Men who at the end of the day actually need a shower because they are covered in dirt. These days, some women have also been hired on in the mines and into construc-tion, but watch a road crew building a road and you will see that America is still mostly manmade. Mr. Trump prefers this vision not because he likes these people—his economic policies would seem to indicate that he does not—but because they are, like coal, seriously solid. The imagination only has to go so far to think a road, a power line, a bridge, a train on its tracks, a massive wall, a lump of coal, the workers who step-by-step twist these into form.

Where the imagination goes, money promises to follow. Mr. Trump, unlike many political leaders, has garnered his modest popularity without (to date) ever funding any of these things, though he has curtailed environmental protections as a means of encouraging industrial expansion of the most material sorts. Tailings may now be let in streams; new leases may now be issued on federal lands unsubject to environmental review: Obama's "Clean Power Plan" undone. These are free gifts to industry. However, promises that require cash on the table—like building and renewing infrastructure or building a border wall or buoying up coal or providing secure employment to the people who labor to bring such things to pass—have seemed sufficient until now. It is enough to hold a thing dear, to supply a vision, and then, Tom Sawyering the deal, pushing others to pony up the funds. Granted, Mexico is balking at the "$10 billion or less" needed for a border wall, and American states and cities are balking at the suggestion that the "$1 trillion" in infrastructure funding promised during the campaign now must come from their own coffers.

These are political problems and fiduciary ones. There will be wrangling. They are also, I hold, secondary to what matters. The imagination—Mr. Trump's imagination, but far from his alone— has been fossil fueled for a long time. It is solidly grounded in the condensed remains of Paleozoic forests.

"Coal, oil, natural gas. 1750–2050." It should read as a gravestone. Coal has already had its day; it no longer stands at the heart of our infrastructure. Oil, more material by far than its natural-gas companion fuel, is also, quiet suddenly, on its way out. Oil already doesn't fuel America's electricity system (says everyone but Hawaii; said everyone but Puerto Rico), but infrastructures of power are not the only thing changing. The cars—the cause célèbre of the contemporary oil industry and the raisons d'être of the national road system—are changing, and when they go their infrastructures will grow all catawampus without them.

Today, 70 percent of the oil used in the world fuels transport. Yet across the globe governments are now turning the great ships of state against these oil-based systems. The internal-combustion engine—internally combusting ocean liners across seas, trucks across continents, cars across town—has quiet suddenly gone from ubiquitous to ignominious.[1] England, for one, is phasing out the internal-combustion engine. No cars will have them on that first industrial isle after 2040. France is following suit but subtracting five years: 2035. China ("no date set") is doing the same. California is now talking about joining this group. As gas wisps away from the engines of the world, it is slowly following coal to the graveyard. At long last the fossils that fuel will be allowed their rest; they will become mere fossils once more.

The end of coal for electricity is further along. In 2016 almost all (93 percent) of the utility-scale power generation added to the American grid was fueled by things difficult to grasp; in fact, 60 percent of it was wind and solar (8.7 GW and 7.7 GW, respectively). Together these two account for twice the infrastructure of new natural gas that year (33 percent or 9 GW). These statistics are just for utility-scale installations, nary a rooftop solar array is included in their number. And these grew by 116 percent in 2016 to 16 gigawatts (GW), "more than doubling the record-breaking 7.3 GW installed in 2015" according to SEIA, a trade organization for the solar industry. And just to trump the chump one last time, today 43 percent of the people working in power in the United States work in the solar sector. That's more than coal, oil, and natural gas combined.

In a way, America is lucky. Much of our infrastructure built up in the midcentury heydays of the president's own youth is reaching the end of its useful life. It's aging out, falling down and to bits. It's blowing down and into shards; it's sinking down under storm surges higher than they ought to be and rain more ferocious than recent memories permit for. Florida didn't just lose power under Irma, she is drowning in shit as sewer systems—never designed to account for that much water—fail. Even without climactic anomalies, massive infrastructure investments are needed to keep America at borderline "great," a level to which we've grown accustomed.

Trump's folly, Florida's folly, is not the act of rebuilding the sewers, roads, bridges, dams, railways, electrical and other cabling that holds this country together. This is both necessary and good. The folly is in rebuilding it as if it were still the 1950s, as if utilities were still government-supported monopolies; as if we didn't have computers and the flexibility, intelligence, connectivity, and interoperability these beget; as if coal were the wisest way to make power and the gas the rightest way to fuel fleets. As if the weather had not already begun to change, the storms grown stronger and the seasons more schizophrenic. In other words, the hardness of coal—a sense of sureness derived from definite, graspable things—is the wrong mnemonic. It betrays the task. With it, we build wrong.

There is a joke about Florida that circulates through green energy circles. Florida, the sunshine state, has one of the lowest sunbeam to solar panel ratios in the country. Instead of using the sun to make power or even encouraging this use among its customers, Florida uses natural gas (61 percent), coal (23 percent), and nuclear (12 percent). Its modest "renewable" power generation (4 percent) is split unequally between a biomass burner—good for getting rid of the excesses of the citrus industry, very bad for global warming—and hydropower. There is one big solar facility and a smattering of rooftop installations, but a close relationship between the state's utilities and its legislature, which sets the laws governing this industry, has meant that solar is arguably the most underutilized resources in a state that suffers inordinate and frequent damage from ocean-born storms.

If anyone should care about decarbonizing their electricity supply, it's Florida. Ranked third among states in solar-power potential and similarly high on the less-august list of states ranked by air-conditioner use, its seems almost criminal that Florida is, in essence, combusting methane to make its swampy lands more livable. Criminal because air conditioners are uniquely suited to solar. They need power during the day; the sun makes power during the day and, voila, a match made in heaven. In Florida, it has also turned out to be a match made far too expensive and complicated by utility and legislative collusion. That's not the joke. That's just the way it is. Here is the joke:

Q: Why don't they have any solar in Florida?

A: Because they'll be underwater before the payback period is over.

It's not very funny, but these days one is given to wonder if it is true.

In Puerto Rico the situation is worse and yet the joke is much the same. The island made its electricity from oil, despite solar resources that put even Florida to shame. Puerto Rico's Hurricane Maria, its storm of the century, flattened all of that with impunity. Its grid is, for all intents and purposes, gone. Its roads remain impassible, and even if they were clear the nation's trucks would not move for there is no fuel to feed them. Its sewers have flooded up over ground, making cesspools of standing water. Its cows scattered and drowned, its people, as if irony were the mover of men, are bound for Florida.

We can blame President Trump for not caring more, not doing more. He deserves this blame. But beyond the immediate, the world he works to support—a world with coal at its heart—is the underlying cause of Maria's extraordinary ferocity.

The electricity system is unique in that it is a central contributor to the climactic systems given to destroying it. We use fossil fuels, including natural gas, to make electricity; the chemical pollution from these adds massively to global warming; global warming makes for more ferocious storms; and these storms swoop in and decimate the grid. This destruction prompts people to think about ways that the grid might be made harder to destroy. Occasionally even, we take action on these thoughts and change some small thing. It is an absurdist loop, inefficient and peculiarly destructive. And yet it is the one we take, not because it's cheaper but because it's easier to think. This is coalthink at its purest and most dismal.

NOTE

1. Airplanes run on gas turbines, similar to gas-fired power plants, no pistons involved; most would say that this is also an internal-combustion engine.

VIOLENCE AND CRIMINAL JUSTICE

PATRICK SHARKEY

O n a rainy day in December of 2013, I visited the Heritage Foundation, one of the country's most prominent conservative think tanks, to talk about how to reform the criminal-justice system. I sat at a long oval table with a politically diverse group of researchers, policy makers, and institutional leaders and discussed what we know about how mass incarceration has affected families, how time in prison alters long-term prospects for stable employment, and how the impact of imprisonment lingers on to affect the next generation. There were moments of disagreement and frustration, but there was one point of virtual consensus. Almost everyone in the room agreed that the scale of incarceration in the United States was unsustainable.

In that year, 2013, the national homicide rate *descended* to its lowest point in at least five decades. And yet more than 2.2 million Americans were imprisoned, and over *four million* more were living under the supervision of the criminal justice system, either on parole or probation.

Before the meeting began, I thought that I would have to spend the day making the case for the damaging consequences of mass incarceration and arguing that the crime decline had changed the nature of the debate on criminal-justice policy. But in fact I faced few challenges throughout the day. After two decades of falling violence, the staggering number of incarcerated Americans seemed misguided to all of us. The tough-on-crime rhetoric that used to dominate discussions of criminal-justice policy in the 1990s had softened, and few contested the harmful consequences of mass incarceration. I left the Heritage Foundation convinced that our nation's long-term reliance on the prison system was coming to an end.

Almost a year into the Trump administration, I'm less certain. This essay explains why.

How We Got Here

The roots of our current criminal-justice system took hold in the 1960s, when debates about the growing crisis in U.S. cities intensified. Cities were the primary settings for a set of social problems that were becoming increasingly visible to the American public, like air and water pollution, economic dislocation, violent crime, and racial unrest. Toward the end of the decade, central city neighborhoods were torn apart by widespread riots and ultimately left behind—their poverty increasingly ghettoized—by a large-scale, long-term migration to the suburbs.

Debates about the "urban crisis" occurred throughout the 1960s, centering on the question of how to understand and how to respond to the challenges posed by concentrated poverty, persistent racial inequality, and violence. One perspective explained these problems as the result of entrenched inequality and injustice, thereby providing the intellectual, moral, and political motivation for legislation leading to major advances in civil rights and an urban agenda centered around investment and empowerment. But over the course of the decade, an alternative perspective linked together antiwar protests, urban riots, and rising violent crime as reflections of growing lawlessness and disorder. This explanation of the urban crisis was laid out most explicitly in Richard Nixon's 1968 presidential campaign, and in his time in office it was translated into an urban-policy agenda characterized by the abandonment of poor urban neighborhoods and the punishment of their residents. Under Nixon, the federal government withdrew resources for cities, expanded support for law enforcement, and pushed the country toward an increasingly punitive criminal justice system.

This model of abandonment and punishment remained largely intact for most of the next fifty years, during both Democratic and Republican administrations. Although ambitious urban programs have been proposed over time, in the decades since Nixon took office there has never been a systematic effort to deal with the problem of urban poverty through sustained, large-scale investments in the nation's urban neighborhoods. Punishment, implemented through state and federal policies that have bolstered the capacity of law enforcement and broadened the reach of the criminal-justice system, has been the most consistent response to the challenges of urban violence and poverty.

By the time I visited the Heritage Foundation, however, this longstanding model seemed to be on the verge of collapsing. While the level of incarceration has grown over time, critics on the Left have consistently pushed back. The calls for criminal-justice reform to counter the injustice of the system and to protect individual rights have only grown stronger over time, fortified by the Black Lives Matter movement and influential books like Michelle Alexander's *The New Jim Crow*. But these are no longer the only voices arguing against the carceral state. As the level of violence has fallen, the calls for harsh punishment that were common in the 1990s have died down, and voices on the right—Newt Gingrich, Rand Paul, even Paul Ryan—have argued for an end to the massive government investments in the prison system, motivated by the principles of antigovernment ideology, fiscal austerity, and even religious redemption.

The new, bipartisan movement for criminal justice reform is visible in public policy. The Second Chance Act, first passed in 2008 and renewed in 2015, was designed to give returning prisoners a better chance to integrate back into society by making it possible for some prisoners convicted of nonviolent offenses to have their records expunged. The Fair Sentencing Act, passed in 2010, addressed the most glaring example of racially biased punishment by reducing the disparities between sentences for crack versus powder cocaine. States as politically and culturally diverse as California, Connecticut, Georgia, and Texas have taken aggressive steps to reduce the size of the incarcerated population while dozens more have passed legislation allowing local jurisdictions to reform their criminal-justice systems and reinvest the savings in programs designed to serve former prisoners more effectively and reduce violence.

A new compromise had emerged by the last years of the Obama administration. Although the federal government still had not made major investments in central-city neighborhoods, there was growing consensus that punishment was not the solution to the challenges of urban poverty. Criminal justice reform seemed inevitable, guided by the ideals of justice, civil rights, faith, liberty, and austerity.

A Turn Backward and a Look Ahead

Close to four years have passed since I sat in the conference room at the Heritage Foundation, and much has changed in the time since. The national homicide rate was close to a historic low at that point, but it rose sharply in 2015 and 2016. Even if most cities haven't seen a meaningful change, the abrupt rise of violence in cities like Baltimore and Chicago provides a reminder of what city life used to be like in much of the country.

Our focus that day was the prison system, but policing has become an equally salient issue in the time since. A series of police shootings caught on camera revealed to the nation how residents of low-income communities of color have been treated for decades, and Black Lives Matter has mobilized a large-scale social movement designed to confront police violence and brutality. President Obama convened a historic task force on policing that called for meaningful changes in the relationship between law enforcement and the communities they serve, and police departments across the country began to implement serious reforms designed to build trust, repair relationships, and confront violence in a new cooperative way guided by the ideals of legitimacy and justice.

And then came the 2016 presidential campaign, the election of Donald Trump, and the appointment of Attorney General Jeff Sessions. President Trump used the recent rise of violence to sow fear in the minds of Americans, citing false statistics on crime and comparing conditions in Chicago to Afghanistan. Trump has taken symbolic steps to undermine the movement for reform, openly endorsing police violence and pardoning former Arizona sheriff Sheriff Joe Arpaio, who was convicted for defying a federal order to end the practice of detaining residents who had not committed any crime but whom he suspected of being undocumented. Sessions has taken active steps to roll back the Obama administration's investigations into civil-rights abuses by police departments; he has ordered prosecutors to pursue the harshest charges available to them; and he recently ended the federal program providing guidance to local agencies seeking to build trust with residents.

President Trump's repeated calls for "law and order" represent a clear turn backward to the rhetoric used by Richard Nixon in 1968. But where does it leave us as we look forward? After a year of President Trump, criminal-justice policy seems likely to move in one of two directions. One possibility is that the long-term, bipartisan movement to scale back the criminal-justice system will continue and the law and order rhetoric coming from Trump and Sessions will come to be seen as an anomalous, unsuccessful, misguided attempt to return to an outdated model of criminal-justice policy. In this scenario, President Trump's abrupt "turn backward" will fade away, and we will continue on the pathway of criminal-justice reform and policing reform in place before the election of 2016.

But a second possibility is that the turn backward to the racialized politics of law and order will gather steam and the movement to scale back the criminal-justice system will lose its momentum. This scenario would mean that the federal government abandons its efforts to scale back its harshest sentencing policies, that state governments end their gradual efforts to reduce incarceration and invest in reentry programs, and that local law-enforcement agencies discontinue their efforts to reduce police violence and build trust among residents of low-income communities of color. Despite the president's disturbing rhetoric and shocking electoral success, this scenario still seems unlikely. The movement to reform policing and criminal justice has continued to move forward, and the reality is that the federal government has little role in criminal-justice policy or in policing, which is decentralized into more than 18,000 local law-enforcement agencies. But the federal government can play a role in leading the way for policy reform, and this scenario may become more likely if the unrest that emerged in the summers of 2015 and 2016 returns or spreads, or if violent crime continues to rise.

I hold out hope for a third scenario, one that continues the progress toward scaling back the prison system and changing the role of law enforcement but also focuses on strengthening urban neighborhoods through local investment. I am not so naïve as to hope for a new federal agenda designed to confront urban inequality. But I am more optimistic about the possibility for a local agenda designed to bolster community organizations, provide extensive supports for returning prisoners, and create stronger relationships among residents, the nonprofit sector, and law enforcement. Even with a president intent on returning to the policies of abandonment and punishment, this type of local agenda is possible because of the growth of competent city leaders from both ends of the political spectrum, a well-developed nonprofit sector, and the growing class of philanthropists who are able to make investments on a scale that is usually unthinkable in the public sector. If we want to reduce the likelihood of a new wave of violence, a local policy agenda focused on justice and investment is essential.

NOTE

Revised May 25, 2018.

WOMEN VOTERS, LEFT AND RIGHT

LINDA GORDON

A Fall 2018 Prelude

When I wrote this short talk many months ago, I was still reeling from the fact that Trump won the presidency despite being recorded saying "grab 'em by the pussy." Perhaps even more I was reeling from learning that a majority of white women voted for him. I listed then some Trump policies that would damage women, and the list gets longer daily. Just a few from my absolutely not comprehensive list: undercutting the Affordable Care Act; reinstating the "gag rule" that prohibits aid to foreign organizations that discuss abortion as a option; allowing medical insurance providers to make maternity coverage optional; ending the Teen Pregnancy Prevention Program; rolling back the 2014 Fair Play and Safe Workplaces Act, banning the Centers for Disease Control and Prevention (CDC) from using the words "fetus," "transgender," and "science-based" . . . Just as important are policies that appear gender neutral but disproportionately hurt women: cutting Medicaid, deregulating drugs, cutting back the supplemental nutrition program for children, allowing government contracts to companies that use forced arbitration of worker complaints, cuts to Meals on Wheels, censoring the State Department's annual human rights report, slashing Section 8 housing vouchers for the homeless . . .

Part of my consciousness about all this was shaped by my examination of 1920s Ku Klux Klan women, of whom there were about 1.5 million. I was so dismayed by learning about this that I wrote a whole chapter in my book about the KKK on "Klan Feminism."[1] Some readers, including friends, disapproved, believed I was wrong to call them feminists. Actually, I've experienced decades of academic discussion about the definition of feminism and when it should be applied as a label. Many believe that a racist can't be *really* a feminist, that antiabortion zealots can't be *truly* feminist, that there cannot be feminists who support imperialism and militarism. I wish this were true, and I'm sad to say that I must disagree. Feminists like me don't own the label. We cannot place an imprimatur on what is correct feminism as the Catholic Church does for books once they're approved by censors. There were KKK women who called for all sorts of women's rights and protections that were not established in the 1920s, such as freedom to divorce, prosecution of wife beaters, equal property rights. Women needed these reforms, and we call them feminist when they're demanded by progressive women. How can we defend the claim that they are not feminist when racist women enunciate them?

All this is importantly related to Trump and Trumpism. Many women voted for him not because they approve of his abusive misogyny but because they have other interests that, pardon the pun, trump their interest in women's rights and safety—interests such as whiteness—and because they accept claims, say, immigrants damage this country, when they are articulated by those they respect. There are female CEOs who are passionate about getting more women into such powerful positions but who also work for corporations that treat their female workers terribly. Hillary Clinton served on Walmart's board of directors; she says she pushed for more women in management and a comprehensive environmental program but not for higher pay and family-friendly schedules for the company's low-income workers—can we therefore conclude that she is not a feminist? The great campaigner for women's rights Elizabeth Cady Stanton was quite willing to accept woman suffrage for elite, educated women only—do we have the right to say she was not a feminist? To write her out of our feminist history?

I'm sure that many, perhaps most pro-Trump women would not call themselves feminists, but that is because the label has been defined not only by "PC" feminists like me but also by antifeminists who consider feminism to be a project of white, elite, antifamily, antimale snobs who call Trump voters stupid and mean. No one owns this word.

Still, there is history. In fact, most women's-rights movements have been progressive on other issues, especially in promoting race and class equality. That's not a matter of definition; it's a matter of what has actually happened in the world.

What follows came from my work as a historian.

Thoughts on Feminism, Trump, and Identity Politics

Just as racism and anti-Semitism nourish each other, as Eric K. Ward says in his "Skin in the Game: How Anti-Semitism Animates White Nationalism," so do racism and antifeminism. Also militarism and antifeminism, homophobia and antifeminism: there are many pairs like these. Value systems that support imperialism, religious bigotry, anti-intellectualism, and individualism—which often boils down to claims that the profit motive is the best, perhaps only force for progress—all these are all mutually nourishing, even mutually constitutive, and all play a role in antifeminism, even misogyny.

I would use Raymond Williams's notion of a "structure of feeling" to characterize these kinships.[2] His concept is particularly apropos at this moment because it directs our attention to attitudes and emotions as political forces themselves, part of an infrastructure that supports political ideologies. These are constructed not only cognitively but also through what sociologist Arlie Hochschild has called "feeling rules."[3] The commonsense understanding of emotions imagines them as individual attributes—as if they had some sort of ur-authenticity—when in fact feelings can be taught just as ideas are—as when schoolchildren learn to feel national pride through reciting the pledge of allegiance or antiabortion discourse "teaches" women to feel guilty after abortions.

I'm not going to try to identify the root or coherence of these structures of feeling. But I do want to make clear that I am pointing not only to Trump's angry core constituency, the people who find satisfaction in Trump's aggressive "fuck you" directed at what they consider the political elite. I am thinking also of his establishment voters and enablers. This in turn requires questioning the journalistic drumbeat that blames his election on a white male working class suffering from deindustrialization. That analysis is not only partial but also seriously misleading, as Nate Silver and numerous others have shown. During the primaries, for example, Trump support came disproportionately from high-income Americans. Although a majority of white working-class men apparently supported Trump in the general election, only 35 percent of Trump supporters had earned less than $50,000 while 53 percent of that income group supported Clinton. Even the much-touted non-college-educated voters were relatively prosperous.[4] An economic explanation—a class analysis—of Trump's victory works less well for his angry, cheering, bullying, and impoverished enthusiasts than for his prosperous supporters, who put up with his braggadocio because they are counting on him to deliver neoliberal policies, namely deregulation and tax cuts.

Trumpism may arise from bitterness and envy, even despair, but the demagoguery directs that anger downward, at the least powerful. If we want to consider Trumpism a form of populism—a label I consider misleading and unuseful, but that is another story[5]—what makes it right-wing populism is that its fury never aims upward at those with political and economic power. Racism, xenophobia, religious intolerance, sexism, misogyny—these structures of feeling have been learned.

But what about female Trump supporters? Many observers who were, like me, inexcusably naïve, expected Trump's crude and abusive behavior to turn away white women—women of color were already hostile to Trump—but it did not. If white women had rejected his sexism as much as people of color rejected his racism, he would of course not be president. For many the motivation for a Trump vote was hostility to Clinton, and women were among these who hated her. Some of that hostility came from sexism, from which women are not immune. But Clinton also represented Wall Street. (My favorite voting instruction, from early in the campaign, was that in a choice between Goldman Sachs and fascism, you have to choose Goldman Sachs.) Better voter data would help us understand which women supported Trump; we don't have class or income data among them, although the fact that so many were college graduates suggests that many were quite prosperous. And we don't yet have the benefit of interviews asking, respectfully, why female Trump supporters were undeterred by his abuse of women.

On the basis of what information we have now, it seems likely that most female Trump supporters do not identify with feminism.

In considering this, bear in mind that feminism has not always been marginal or far left. For example, in 1974 the majority polled by Roper said that they approved of feminism; in 1989, 78 percent of women polled by CNN/*Time* did so, and a third called themselves feminists.[6] Today, six in ten women and one-third of men self-identify as feminist.[7] What we are confronting is a large minority's rage against feminism, revved up by media that have labeled feminists as "feminazis." The antifeminist rage is, in turn, a facet of the multivalent anger fueled by the demagoguery and falsehoods of right-wing talk shows and social media.

For this many share the blame. The media from which right-wingers get their information; the ministers and priests who make opposition to abortion and gay marriage their top priority; the schools that don't teach the history of feminism; the Democratic Party leaders who derided welfare and taxes and allied with Wall Street; the journalists—including liberal ones—who misrepresented feminism by focusing disproportionately on issues such as rape, abortion, and sexual harassment while neglecting feminist campaigns for equal pay, jobs and promotions, family leave, prenatal care, athletic opportunities, and much more.

Some of the blame attaches to we feminists ourselves. The 1960s and 1970s feminist revival grew first from labor unions and the Old Left, then from civil rights and the New Left. Feminists continued the commitment to collective action they imbibed from these roots. Feminism was then—as it was historically—a political ideology and strategy. More recently its most visible streams are redefining it as an assertion of individual ambition and lifestyle choice. (The development of "choice" as the slogan for abortion rights prefigured that transformation.) In the current vernacular, "feminism" is often merely a label for individual determination and assertiveness, expressed through working harder or working out or eating healthily. Some, like the philosopher Nancy Fraser, call it neoliberal feminism, thereby embedding the transformation in global developments. The journalist Andi Zeisler refers to the marketization and celebrity-ization of feminism, although she acknowledges that something is gained when, say, Beyoncé declares herself a feminist.[8] But when feminism is identified primarily with cool celebrities and corporate ambition, it is small wonder that many women don't see it as useful to them.

Let me add a corollary hypothesis: that the less-wealthy female Trump supporters are pessimistic. Despite the ideology that anyone can "make it" or that luck might happen, many in Trump's base aren't hopeful. Their neighbors are often strung out on meth or opioids, beset by obesity and other disabilities. There is a particularly female, private version of the absence of hope: the conclusion that we women just have to put up with men's disrespect. When I wrote about domestic violence I saw how often abused women were told by other women "that's the way men are." It's not that female Trump supporters like seeing women humiliated, but they may lack confidence that men can learn to behave better. Some may even interpret abusive behavior as a sign of strength and confidence. By contrast, feminism, far from man hating, rests on confidence that men can change. And they have evidence: for example, when Trump's predatory braggadocio was excused as "only locker room talk," none of the men I knew reported ever hearing such talk in locker rooms. Feminist optimism was particularly strong in the New Left generation because we saw men and women change and become happier in the process.

None of this lets the Democratic Party off the hook. Obama, whose intelligence and careful speaking were balm for liberal intellectuals, bailed out Wall Street at the expense of cutbacks in collective social provision and deported millions. These policies function as cause as well as effect: they feed the myth that people of color and immigrants are getting ahead because of handouts. A single-payer federal health-insurance plan, which was ruled out at the beginning of drafting Obamacare, might have counteracted some of this: precisely because it would have been universal, it could have alleviated the impression that the middle class was subsidizing the poor. Lily Geismer's *Don't Blame Us: Suburban Liberals and the Transformation of the Democratic Party* shows in part how the party began to represent millionaire donors and prosperous suburbanites, "affluent knowledge professionals," rather than working-class or low-income people.[9] All these factors helped move feminism away from its social movement roots.

Amidst the collateral damage of Trumpism is the resuscitation of an old intra-Left strategic division that feminism tried to bury: between "identity politics" and an allegedly universal economic appeal. Some left-of-center magazines and social media are denouncing Clinton and the Democratic Party for focusing on racism, sexism, and xenophobia. They call this "identity politics," which is code for black, Latino/a, women's, and LGBTQ movements. (As if billionaires and white nationalists don't have their own "identity politics.") They argue for a strategy that focuses on economic policies, remaining silent regarding racism and sexism in the hope that doing so will win over the "white working class."

Much is wrong with that strategy. It rests on the assumption that the white working class was primarily responsible for Trump's victory. It rests equally on the assumption that a successful progressive economic appeal to that group would tamp down the racist and sexist furies that drove the 2016 election. (For some, that assumption derives from a simplistic "Marxist" idea that racism and sexism are mere epiphenomena of class exploitation.) Runaway shops (a.k.a. globalization), deindustrialization, and automation have made "working class" more and more an abstraction, no longer a shared position among lower-income people. Then there's the most important defense of so-called identity politics:

that racism and sexism will ultimately undermine any struggle against inequality. We don't have the luxury to choose between "identity" and economic issues; they are inextricably entangled. Worse, the call to scrap "identity politics" only feeds the racism and sexism being revved up by Trumpism.

Perhaps worst, the either/or binary ignores one of the most important lessons of social movements: that progressive strategies need to ally with people in motion, such as Black Lives Matter, the Dreamers, Fight for $15, and campus campaigns against rape, as well as those campaigning to get rid of statues and building mottos honoring defenders of slavery.

In this regard it bears noting that the "identity politics" concept derives from this strategic understanding. First used by the Combahee River Collective, an African American socialist feminist group, in a 1977 manifesto, it expressed the premise that "the most profound and potentially most radical politics come directly out of our own identity, as opposed to working to end somebody else's oppression." One might add, the most effective politics.

NOTES

Revised August 8, 2018.
1. Linda Gordon, *The Second Coming of the KKK: the Ku Klux Klan and the American Political Tradition* (New York: Liverlight, 2017).
2. Raymond Williams, a great British social and cultural critic, first used this phrase in *A Preface to Film* (1954), then elaborated it in his later books *The Long Revolution* and *Marxism and Literature*. He uses "structure of feeling" as a concept that argues for the material reality of culture, but employs the term "feeling" in order to "emphasize a distinction from more formal concepts of 'world view' or 'ideology.' . . . We are talking about characteristic elements of impulse, restraint, and tone; specifically affective elements of consciousness and relationships: not feeling against thought, but thought as felt and feeling as thought: practical consciousness of a present kind, in a living and interrelating continuity. We are then defining these elements as a 'structure': as a set, with specific, internal relations, at

once interlocking and in tension." Williams, *Marxism and Literature* (Oxford: Oxford University Press, 1977), 132. This concept is related to another Williams theorization: cultural materialism.

3. Arlie Russell Hochschild, *The Managed Heart: Commercialization of Human Feeling* (Berkeley: University of California Press, 1983).

4. For example, a March 2016 NBC survey (http://www.msnbc.com/msnbc /why-trumps-appeal-wider-you-might-think) showed that only a third of Trump supporters had household incomes at or below the national median of about $50,000. Another third made $50,000 to $100,000, and the other third made $100,000 or more. And that was true even when we limited the analysis to only non-Hispanic whites. The report's authors confirmed these findings again just days after the election (https://www .washingtonpost.com/news/monkey-cage/wp/2017/06/05/its-time-to -bust-the-myth-most-trump-voters-were-not-working-class/). See also Skye Gould and Rebecca Harrington, "Seven Charts Show Who Propelled Trump to Victory," *Business Insider*, November 10, 2016, http://www .businessinsider.com/exit-polls-who-voted-for-trump-clinton-2016-11.

5. See my "What Do We Mean by Populism?" *Perspectives*, American Historical Association (September 2017).

6. Karlyn H. Keene, "Feminism vs. Women's Rights," in *The Public Perspective* (November–December 1991), https://ropercenter.cornell.edu/public -perspective/ppscan/31/31003.pdf, quoting from a variety of polls.

7. Weiyi Cai and Scott Clement, "What Americans Think About Feminism Today," *Washington Post*, January 27, 2016, https://www.washingtonpost .com/graphics/national/feminism-project/poll/, data from a *Washington Post*/Kaiser Family Foundation poll.

8. Nancy Fraser, *Fortunes of Feminism: From State-Managed Capitalism to Neoliberal Crisis* (London: Verso, 2013); Andi Zeisler, *We Were Feminists Once: From Riot Grrrl to CoverGirl, the Buying and Selling of a Political Movement* (New York: Public Affairs, 2016).

9. Lily Geismer, *Don't Blame Us: Suburban Liberals and the Transformation of the Democratic Party* (Princeton, NJ: Princeton University Press, 2015). Bias-check disclosure: the book appeared in a series that I coedit.

THE OFFICE OF THE PRESIDENCY

ROBERT SHRUM

To borrow a phrase from his own reckless comment on North Korea, Donald Trump has debased the office of the presidency to an extent "like the world has never seen." His policies are capricious, often cruel, and potentially disastrous. But there is something rotten in the state of Trump that goes beyond even that. He is uniquely—among American presidents—unstable, small-minded, and malevolent. In this he has company in some past occupants of the Oval Office; unlike them, he has no offsetting merits on the other side of the ledger.

In reporting on his policies, the media continually heralds a pivot that might push this Frankenstein presidency within shouting distance of normalcy. For months, every time someone wrote that Trump was pivoting, he usually turned 360 degrees. Then, in September, he made a deal with "Chuck and Nancy" on the debt ceiling that actually will cede real power to Democrats when the ceiling has to be raised again in a few months, with the country on the brink of a default that could trigger a global economic crisis. He also made half a deal on DACA and the "dreamers," although his recent hard-line demands likely mean that "bipartisan" dalliance may never be consummated.

The *Wall Street Journal*'s headline was typical: "Trump's Pivot? His Job Is to Get Things Done." The temptation to normalize Trump is understandable. No one wants a president—constantly shadowed by a military officer carrying the nuclear codes—who is preternaturally weird and provokes a *Politico* story entitled "When Aides Worry Their President Is Unhinged."

It's not that the Oval Office has invariably been the province of the levelheaded and the well balanced. Lyndon Johnson may have been "paranoid" and "depressed," with "an unfillable hole in his ego," as his close aide Bill Moyers said. His successor, Richard Nixon, was not only corrupt but indisputably paranoid, too, frequently perusing his "enemies list" and, in his final days, pumped full of pills, reportedly prowling the halls at night talking to the portraits of his predecessors. But Johnson and Nixon were at least competent—and in many ways well beyond simply competent—and while both protracted the catastrophe of the Vietnam war, each had masterful gifts that, in other arenas, led to historic achievements.

Donald Trump has shown no evidence of any such compensatory talent. The pivots currently ascribed to him are almost certainly driven more by animus toward the Republican leadership of the Senate and the House than any thought-out strategy and can hardly elide the substantive damage he has already inflicted on the nation and the world.

The seven months he has been in office feel like seven years or more: the Paris climate accord repudiated and environmental safeguards shredded; equal rights rolled back and voting rights threatened; consumer rights subverted and a hard-right ideologue appointed to the Supreme Court; the Muslim ban gleefully proclaimed in week one and relations frayed with vital allies like Britain and Germany. The list could go on and on, extending to the possibilities of collusion with Russia during the 2016 election, obstruction of justice, and financial dealings that violate the Constitution and the law.

I suspect all this will end badly—for Trump or for us, or more likely for both Trump and us. But even as this saga plays out, we know already that he has also inflicted less tangible but grievous wounds on the American spirit.

I have argued elsewhere that one standard of greatness in presidents is whether they "define, redefine, and enlarge the scope of our national identity." In modern times, Franklin Roosevelt, John F. Kennedy, and Ronald Reagan left indelible imprints on America's conception of itself, lifting our vision of what we could and should aspire to. Even those who disagreed with Reagan on many issues cannot deny that at a troubled time he renewed the country's confidence in itself. Kennedy not only lifted our eyes toward space but, through establishing the Peace Corps and other programs, inspired generations of activism that have led America closer to fulfilling its ideals.

Other presidents have also sought to meet this standard. It wasn't the way to do it, but Nixon tellingly if awkwardly paraphrased Kennedy in his 1968 acceptance address when he celebrated "not what government did for people—but . . . what people did for themselves." He inverted Kennedy's meaning, but at least he tried. And at his best, Barack Obama succeeded, offering an eloquent and resonant narrative—indeed, he embodied it—about the better country we could become.

Words have power—for good or ill. In his language and in his appeal to Americans' darker impulses, Trump not only debases the presidency, but he deliberately sets out an ugly vision of a nasty, narrower America, fearful of "the other," intolerant and closing in on itself. His stubborn insistence that "both sides" were to blame in Charlottesville is a prime example. Whether he believes this or whether he is attempting simply to satisfy the basest part of his base, what message does it send to soft-pedal a condemnation of neo-Nazis and white supremacists? What message does it send when he calls Mexicans "rapists" and then "bad hombres"—or when he mocks a disabled reporter?

The lies, the incitements, the demonization of the press and his opponents, the misogyny and xenophobia flow from Donald Trump in a tidal wave and could wash away long years of progress toward "liberty and justice for all." Warren Harding, probably no longer at risk of being rated our worst president, once said: "I like to go out in the woods and bloviate." Trump bloviates endlessly on Twitter; in 280 characters and in rhetoric that traffics in phrases like "American carnage" and "America first," he invites people not to build a nation that is truly "great again" but to retreat to a less grand and less decent land.

He expresses his anti-vision in an infantile vocabulary. Some conclude that this is a political advantage. The MIT professor Edward Schiappa, while arguing that Trump's "words suggest a very simplistic mind that may not be up to the challenges of the presidency in the 21st century," allows that his "plain style . . . probably accounts for Trump's popularity among the less educated citizens who prefer the sort of simplicity we saw from George Bush." But Roosevelt, Kennedy, and Reagan had no trouble reaching people—even those Schiappa calls "the less educated"—while at the same time inspiring hope and instilling a sense of honorable or even noble mission. Instead of speaking down to Americans, a president can lift them up.

So the response to Trump cannot be a descent to his level. His juvenile language of malevolence, his reactionary conception of America, must be answered with a language of ideals that speaks to our better selves and challenges the country to reach higher. Think of conservatives like John McCain or like Nebraska senator Ben Sasse, who never endorsed Trump in 2016 and recently rebuked him for "weaponizing distrust." Or think of Democratic representative Joe Kennedy III, who lit up social media recently when he told an audience in Austin, Texas: "This is our story, our message, our electoral strategy, and our moral responsibility. To rebuild a country defined by the decency it offers every proud man, woman, or child blessed to call this nation home. Where strength isn't measured by who you prey on, but who you protect. Where greatness isn't just a show of muscle, but of mercy."

Whatever the daily twists and turns of this mad Trumpian misadventure, the challenge in response is to heed Lincoln and summon "the better angels of our nature." This is essential to restoring and resuming the upward arc of the American journey. Over three-quarters of a century, from FDR to Obama, it's been the right thing to do—and more often than not, the right way to win.

NOTE

Revised May 25, 2018.

RELIGION AND THE REPUBLIC

PHILIP GORSKI

I still remember reading Tocqueville's *Democracy in America* for the first time as a freshman in college. I was astonished! How could this French aristocrat have understood us so well, I wondered. And how could we have changed so little over such a long period of time?

Last week, I reread Tocqueville's other, lesser-known masterwork, *The Old Regime and the French Revolution*. I was astonished all over again. How could Trump's America be so much like Tocqueville's France? How could we have changed so much in the last thirty-five years?

Let me explain what is at stake, the problems that we face, and how we can confront them, all from a Tocquevillean point of view. What is at stake is the American creed of freedom, equality, inclusion, and solidarity. What is endangering it is the growing animosity between religious and nonreligious Americans and the growth of tribalism on both the Left and the Right. What is needed is a unifying vision that draws Americans together again without whitewashing the differences that divide them. But also new policies to regenerate civic unity.

In *Democracy in America*, Tocqueville observed that religion and republicanism had always gone hand in hand in the United

States and to the benefit of both. Not because church and state were merged or because the clergy meddled in politics but precisely because they weren't and didn't. There was no established religion and the clergy maintained a respectful distance from politics. Still, religion provided a powerful buttress to republican government. The churches schooled Americans in the practice of voluntary association while the clergy gently instilled respect for the nation's laws. Not always, of course, but in their better moments at least.

In France, on the other hand, religion and republicanism were increasingly at odds with each other and to the detriment of both. The rupture between religion and republicanism during the revolution was succeeded by a bad marriage between religion and empire consecrated by Napoleon. There was an official religion, and the clergy was politically vocal. In this ill-fated union between throne and altar, the Catholic Church supported the French monarchy while the clergy preached obedience to authority, and republicans therefore opposed both. This same dynamic played out across all of Latin Europe. In these countries, it was politics rather than science that really drove people out of the churches.

Having discerned the likely outcome of these dynamics early on, Tocqueville sagely advised that "Religion by uniting with different political powers, can . . . form only burdensome alliances. It has no need of their help to survive and may die, if it serves them."

The religious right in Trump's America would do well to heed Tocqueville's advice. Since the late 1970s it has embraced the Republican Party ever more tightly, alienating increasing numbers of Americans from Christianity. For a time, the adverse effects of the evangelical-Republican alliance on American Christianity were concealed by high birth rates among religious conservatives. But then, last year, a number of evangelical leaders made a Faustian bargain with Donald Trump: their moral credibility in exchange for promises of political protection. As a result, the day of reckoning is coming and coming soon.

Some evangelical leaders have taken a principled stand against this bargain, in effect a suicide pact, and rightly so. Christian intellectuals such as Russell Moore and Peter Wehner have spoken out forcefully against Trumpism, and they are paying a heavy price for doing so. But the price for the evangelical churches will be heavier still. The inevitable result will be the continued secularization of American society—and also the rapid fragmentation of the evangelical movement.

The evangelical community is already splintering along existing fault lines of generation, gender, and race. Younger evangelicals who care about environmental stewardship and social justice, evangelical women disgusted by the hypocritical double standards of male clergymen, and nonwhite evangelicals angered by the abominations of white nativism are increasingly uneasy with their national leadership, even at evangelical strongholds such as Wheaton College and Liberty University. If the national spokesmen of the religious right ignore these warnings—as it appears they will—then they are destined to repeat history—*French* history.

The coming crisis of the religious right could be an opportunity for the progressive left. From the revolution to abolition to civil rights, reformist movements in the United States have succeeded only if and to the degree that they have assembled diverse coalitions that included people of faith. As Tocqueville knew, and modern social science research confirms, religious communities can generate levels of moral commitment and social capital that secular movements often cannot. The potential power of such an alliance is already on full display in the Moral Mondays movement that has so effectively challenged the populist right in North Carolina.

Building alliances is never easy. In this case it will require that secular progressives and religious moderates agree to disagree on the issues that divide them so that they can work together on the issues that unite them. Many moderate Catholics and alienated evangelicals are ready to lock arms with secular progressives on issues like climate-change policy, the mass-incarceration crisis, and immigration reform. Most accept gay marriage as well. But abortion rights are still a sticking point. This is where secular progressives might need to give a little ground or at least strike a somewhat less strident and more conciliatory tone by acknowledging the very real moral concerns that many people of faith have about "the life questions." Not all prolife Christians are closet antifeminists.

If *Democracy in America* contains important lessons for the religious right, *The Old Regime* should be required reading for the Davos left. One of the most important causes of the French Revolution, Tocqueville argues, was the political abdication of the French aristocracy. The aristocracy did not renounce its privileges—its freedom from taxation—only its responsibilities. When it fled the drudgery of the provinces for the splendors of the court, it ceased to govern, but it did not cease to exploit. On the contrary, disconnected from the daily sufferings of the rural population, it squeezed the last centime out of the peasantry in order to support its idle pleasures. In the long run, says Tocqueville, this arrangement was untenable, making the revolution inevitable.

The American aristocracy of today operates in much the same fashion as the French aristocracy of yesteryear. From its exclusive bastions in the coastal metropolises, it uses financial engineering to squeeze dollars from an ever-expanding debtor class via interest payments and service fees, and it deploys its coding prowess to "disrupt" the lives and livelihoods of taxi drivers, sales clerks, and other lesser mortals. The once vibrant towns and cities of the great industrial heartland that stretches from the Central Valley to the Hudson Valley have been left to languish and decay.

Of course, the new aristocracy does not explicitly base its claims to privilege on birth and culture. Instead, it points to smarts and effort—to Ivy League diplomas and long work weeks—though in truth its privileges have as much to do with accidents of birth and access to culture as anything else. As currently constituted, the American meritocracy mostly reproduces privilege. In the long run, this arrangement is clearly untenable. Sooner or later, a few class traitors and populist tribunes like Donald Trump and Steve Bannon will explain all of this to those left behind. And to great political effect, as we saw in the recent elections.

So why are downscale Americans continually voting against their material interests? After all, it is clear that Trump & Co. will betray their base whenever it suits them. But the real puzzle here is why secular progressives are so puzzled in the first place. They are missing a key lesson from the sociology of religion. For most people, belonging trumps maximizing. Economic self-interest is less powerful than many progressives like to imagine. And appeals to common vision and universal values are more powerful.

So why haven't secular progressives countered Trumpian populism with an alternative vision?

This brings us to a second parallel between pre-revolutionary France and post-Trumpian America. Even as education made the better classes more and more alike, Tocqueville observed, they tried harder and harder to distinguish themselves from one another. They sought solace for their sameness in the finest of distinctions. Closed off from one another in a thousand water-tight compartments, he noted, in so many self-enclosed social niches, all fully isolated from the great unwashed, they first lost the habit of democratic association, then of civic leadership, and finally of mutual sympathy.

Can we not observe an analogous development in contemporary America? The educated middle classes have become more and more alike in their tastes and habits, and the old differences of race, ethnicity, and region have been gradually eroded—a welcome development, of course, for which they continually congratulate themselves. But this sameness conflicts with the bourgeois-bohemian ethos of individualism and authenticity. So they try harder and harder to differentiate themselves from one another by means of the finest differences in taste—be it in hobbies, travel, sports, food, or clothing.

This process of splitting and clustering has been further accelerated in recent years by the advent of social media and consumer capitalism, which allow for the identification and display of ever more fine-grained cultural distinctions. Meanwhile, class contempt grows apace, aggravating existing resentments. Should we be surprised that some Americans react against this preening individualism and yearn for cultural unity, even if they too often find it in all the wrong places?

The university-based intelligentsia is not the prime mover behind these trends. But it has more often abetted than resisted them. The celebration of diversity on American college campuses is now well into its fourth decade. Multiculturalism began as a worthy battle for the cultural recognition of marginalized groups. Yet it has slowly given rise to something else: a utopian crusade to eradicate "cultural insensitivity" of any kind that all too often devolves into scapegoating and witch hunts.

Meanwhile, the populist right has exploited the excesses of the cultural left with considerable success. Some Christian conservatives now present themselves as the most persecuted minority in America. Political performance artists such as Ann Coulter and Milo Yiannopoulos camouflage themselves as civil libertarians. And—most worryingly of all—white nationalists now claim that they are just "defending their culture." In all these ways, the multicultural tribalism of the left has unwittingly provided political cover for the monocultural tribalism of the Right.

The republic is in crisis. That crisis is full of danger but also of opportunity. The danger is that the populist right will further undermine our democratic institutions. But this gives the progressive left an opportunity to articulate an alternative vision of American patriotism. Not the sort of jingoistic and chauvinistic hyperpatriotism that currently travels under the alias of "American exceptionalism"; rather, the sort of critical but affirmative patriotism articulated by leaders like Lincoln and King. A patriotism that also recognizes the universal significance of the American project, namely: to forge a nation of nations and a people of peoples, a continental republic uniting a diverse citizenry around a shared vision of the common good. Such a patriotism could also appeal to political moderates and perhaps even to disaffected Republicans, thereby reversing the rightward drift of the political center.

One of the central insights of Tocqueville's writings—perhaps *the* central insight—is that democratic institutions alone are not sufficient to sustain self-government. Democratic mores are also crucial: habits of association, cooperation, and mutual aid. In early America, Tocqueville observed, these habits were instilled in civil society and especially in religious society. In contemporary America, where commerce crowds out civic life and collective religiosity is giving way to individual spirituality—even in church—they must be acquired elsewhere. But where? This is a vital question for anyone who is concerned about the long-term health of the American republic.

Let me conclude with a few proposals, some modest, others much less so, about how we might renew America's old "habits of the heart." We might start by making civic holidays into holidays again, days when Americans neither work nor shop, days for civic activity and reflection. Second, we could require that every American high school student pass the same civics exam that aspiring citizens take. Third and finally, we could institute a year of national service for all young Americans: no waivers and no exceptions. Together, these measures would go some distance to mending the widening tears in the social fabric of American life. Or, we could continue along the road we are on, a road paved with distraction, disinterest, and disengagement, a road that leads to the not-so-soft tyranny of right-wing populism.

EVANGELICAL VOTERS

TANYA MARIE LUHRMANN

In the 2016 U.S. presidential election over 80 percent of white evangelicals voted for Donald Trump—more even than for Mitt Romney in 2012 or for John McCain in 2008.[1] Candidate Hillary Clinton had her flaws, but she was undeniably a Christian. Donald Trump, not so much. As an anthropologist who has spent many years among evangelical Christians, I have fielded the questions of many flummoxed secular liberals in the past eleven months. How could people of faith, they ask, vote for a philandering liar with the moral compass of a gutter rat?

These secular liberals often assume that evangelical Christians would vote only for Christians and, indeed, only for Christians with upstanding personal lives. This makes sense. In 2011, over 60 percent of these voters had insisted that an official who behaved immorally in their personal life could not fulfill their public duties.[2] Secular liberals might assume from this, however, that evangelicals have simplistic moral views. They'd be wrong.

The choice was likely strategic, although this is not the end of the story. The 2016 election would determine the course of the Supreme Court for many more years than a president would be in office. Voters who believe that abortion is murder and that homosexuality is a sin or that individuals should take responsibility for their own life choices and not rely on government "handouts" probably care a lot about Supreme Court appointments.

For such voters it was quite reasonable to cast their ballots against a Christian candidate who would have put liberals on the bench and for a candidate who—however unreliable he was as a person—was highly likely to appoint conservatives. And indeed, in exit polls, many white evangelicals who said that they voted for Trump spoke about his promise to appoint a Supreme Court judge who would overturn *Roe vs. Wade*.[3] And the number of those who said that immoral behavior in one's private life did not prevent one from fulfilling public responsibilities jumped to 72 percent.

Yet we know that many white evangelical Christians struggled over the evident moral failings of the man. Some pastors spoke out against him. Some public figures endorsed him, unendorsed him, and endorsed him again. For these people the vote was not an easy moral choice.

Two powerful biblical narratives seem to have helped conflicted Christians come to terms with such a man. The first is the narrative of the flawed vehicle. Such figures litter the Hebrew Bible. Adam bit into that apple. Noah got drunk and lay naked in his tent. Moses took credit for finding a miraculous well, and so God refused to let him enter the promised land. David, the greatest king of Israel, was almost Trump-like in his lust and impulses.

In the famous story, David skips out on a battle and, while his men are fighting, spies on a woman bathing naked. He learns that she is married, but he forces her to have sex with him anyway. He can do this because her husband is one of those fighting. When the woman tells him she is pregnant, he first brings the husband back and tries to get the man to sleep with her, so the man will assume that the child is his. But the man is too righteous to have sex when the men under his command are fighting. So David deliberately sends him back to the front of the battle to get him killed. He does this so that no one discovers his own adultery. Yet the Bible tells us that David is a man after the Lord's own heart. Acts 13:22: "[God] raised up unto them David to be their king; to whom also he gave their testimony, and said, I have found David the son of Jesse, a man after mine own heart, which shall fulfil all my will."

Biblical stories wallow in these imperfections. They illustrate God's ability to work his will in the world in mysterious ways. During the presidential campaign, a number of evangelical pastors compared Trump to David.[4] Rick Perry said with characteristic clarity: "You know the good lord used King David. The best I can tell, King David wasn't perfect either. But he was the chosen man of God. Let's go make America great again."[5]

Trump's sheer improbableness as a candidate, up against apparently anointed favorites like Jeb Bush and Marco Rubio, is taken by many Christian observers to be in itself a sign that he was chosen by God. The pastor Paula White: "For me, that has to be providence. That has to be the hand of God."[6] And once you focus in on imperfection as sin, we can none of us throw stones. Psalm 103:3: "If you, Lord, should mark iniquities, Oh Lord, who could stand?"

The second biblical narrative that lays the groundwork for Trump's ascendance is the idea that Jesus will return to remake the world and that the period just before he appears will be marked by chaos and looming catastrophe. This is often known as the "end times." Many evangelical Christians think we are living in it now.[7] North Korea, Harvey, Irma, Maria, wildfires, earthquakes, a hundred-year drought. Add to this Scott Pruitt, health care, and people making terrible decisions divorced from reality, and even liberals feel a sense of coming apocalypse. I have conversations with people who think that humans won't survive on earth beyond their great-grandchildren. If you are a biblical literalist—about a quarter of Americans are—the picture is even more stark.[8]

You might think of the "end times" as a crackpot concept out of Revelation, a book that seems based on a trance vision and is as out of place in the New Testament as the Song of Songs is in the Hebrew Bible. But the idea that Jesus's return will be preceded by calamity can be supported by passages throughout the Scriptures. If you google "end times sign" you will find many identifying features of the period that will presage the moment when God's wrath will wipe the planet clean of the unworthy and create a new age.[9] BeliefNet, a relatively calm and ecumenical site, gives you these:

> Matthew 24:5–8: war, famine, earthquakes. (Think Afghanistan and Mexico City.)
>
> Matthew 24:24: false prophets—charismatic Christians who draw many followers but are corrupt. (Many charismatic Christians think that many of these exist. After Joel Osteen's megachurch apparently failed to open its doors for Houston residents displaced by Harvey, he surely must seem like a contender.)
>
> 2 Timothy 3:1–4: people will be more brutal, heartless, greedy, and proud. (Washington. The 1 percent.)
>
> Luke 21: 25–6: signs in the stars. (Eclipse, anyone? Although the site tells us that this might include missiles, rockets, and bombs.)

Reading the list you could be forgiven for thinking: check, check, check, check. And if the end times are upon us, who cares what happens in Washington?

Are there hopeful signs? The anthropologist Roy D'Andrade once argued that cultural models—the shared schemas that guide the way we make sense of and act in the world—are often implicit. We don't always know why we like this kind of person and dislike that kind. We just do.[10] But put enough pressure on those emotional responses, and the schemas begin to become more clear. Then people recognize their own biases, and things can change. When entire NFL teams bent their knees, some people found that their great dislike of Colin Kaepernick's protest turned into pride at the nation's long history of civil rights.[11] There are signs that ever more Christians are finding it difficult to interpret Trump as God's chosen vehicle.[12] Perhaps it is not yet a movement. But it could be.

Meanwhile, what can a secular liberal do?

For a start, put aside your preconceptions and talk with people you don't understand. A few weeks ago, at a local dinner party, my neighbor Sunny announced that she had decided that her primary political commitment in the coming months was to connect to one conservative each day. She wasn't planning to argue with them or to change their minds. She just wanted to have a conversation so that each of them would be human to the other. Sunny is aggressively activist. She marches in protests. She holds political fund raisers. But she thinks that the central problem in our country has to do with our social fabric. She thinks that we can repair it one by one.

Go ahead, you smug cynics. Laugh. I think she is on to something. Our social science tells us that people are more likely to change their minds on social issues like gay marriage if they know someone from the disdained category.[13] If each of us followed her lead, we might make a difference.

This assumes that end times have not arrived and that we are not blown up in a nuclear holocaust, which I regret to say seems less unlikely than it did not too long ago.

NOTES

1. Gregory A. Smith and Jessica Martínez, "How the Faithful Voted: A Preliminary 2016 Analysis," Pew Research Center, November 9, 2016, http://www.pewresearch.org/fact-tank/2016/11/09/how-the-faithful-voted-a-preliminary-2016-analysis/.

2. Thomas B. Edsall, "Trump Says Jump. His Supporters Ask, How High?," *New York Times*, September 14, 2017, https://www.nytimes.com/2017/09/14/opinion/trump-republicans.html.

3. Sara Bailey, "Exit Polls Show White Evangelicals Voted Overwhelmingly for Donald Trump," *Washington Post*, November 9, 2016, https://www.washingtonpost.com/news/acts-of-faith/wp/2016/11/09/exit-polls-show-white-evangelicals-voted-overwhelmingly-for-donald-trump/.

4. Colby Itkowitz, "'Raised Up by God': Televangelist Paula White Compares Trump to Queen Esther," *Washington Post*, August 23, 2017, https://www.washingtonpost.com/news/acts-of-faith/wp/2017/08/23/raised-up-by-god-televangelist-paula-white-compares-trump-to-queen-esther/.

5. Bill Hoffmann, "Rick Perry Likens Trump to King David as 'Chosen Man of God,'" *Newsmax*, August 2, 2017, http://www.newsmax.com/Newsmax-Tv/rick-perry-trump-king-david/2017/08/02/id/805313/.

6. Lauren Markoe, "Did God Choose Trump? What It Means to Believe in Divine Intervention," *Religion News Service*, January 17, 2017, http://religionnews.com/2017/01/17/did-god-choose-trump-what-belief-in-divine-intervention-really-means/.

7. Gabriel Campanario, "Donald Trump, the Herald of Evangelicals' End Times," *Seattle Times*, September 30, 2016, https://www.seattletimes.com/opinion/donald-trump-the-herald-of-evangelicals-end-times/.

8. Lydia Saad, "Record Few Americans Believe Bible Is Literal Word of God," *Gallup News*, May 15, 2017, http://news.gallup.com/poll/210704/record-few-americans-believe-bible-literal-word-god.aspx.

9. The Jehovah's Witnesses website provides one of the longer lists.

10. Roy D'Andrade, *The Development of Cognitive Anthropology* (Cambridge: Cambridge University Press, 1995).

11. Bryan Flaherty, "From Kaepernick Sitting to Trump's Fiery Comments: NFL's Anthem Protests Have Spurred Discussion," *Washington Post*, September 24, 2017, https://www.washingtonpost.com/graphics/2017/sports/colin-kaepernick-national-anthem-protests-and-NFL-activism-in-quotes; Savannah Haas, "Why I Changed My Mind About Colin

Kaepernick," *State Press*, October 3, 2016, http://www.statepress.com/article/2016/10/spopinion-why-i-changed-my-mind-about-colin-kaepernick.

12. Nancy Hightower, "Christian Resistance to Trump Is Growing," *Huffington Post*, August 29, 2017, https://www.huffingtonpost.com/entry/christian-resistance-to-trump-is-growing_us_598f68e1e4b0caa1687a6096.

13. Jim A. C. Everett, "Intergroup Contact Theory: Past, Present, and Future," *Inquisitive Mind*, no. 17, http://www.in-mind.org/article/intergroup-contact-theory-past-present-and-future.

GUN CULTURE

HAREL SHAPIRA

The day after the Las Vegas shooting, Mark Romano called me up to tell me that Donald Trump was bad for his business. "Don't get me wrong, I love him," Mark clarified, reiterating his earlier comments about how Trump was "a genius" and how Trump "gets the common man, people like me." But for his business, Mark continued, "It sucks him being president."

Mark's business is teaching people how to use guns. And over the past three years I have spent time with people like Mark— talking to them, going to shooting ranges with them, and taking firearms classes with them—in order to understand the role that guns play in contemporary America.

I first met Mark nearly fifteen years ago. Although we were both living in the Northeast at the time—me in New York and Mark in Philadelphia—we met in the middle of the Arizona desert. I was there as a graduate student doing research for my PhD dissertation on militia groups patrolling the border. Mark was there as a member of one of those militia groups. "I'm here because I love my country," Mark told me back then, his patriotic project aligned with a xenophobic one. "I'm here to stop the illegals from invading my country," he said. The threat the "illegals" posed was for Mark at once symbolic and actual. "No one speaks English in this country anymore," he would often say and then shift from this ostensible cultural assault to a physical one. "They are a bunch of hardened criminals who will slit your throat without thinking twice."

For Mark, personal identity and national identity are enmeshed in each other; his sense of personal pride is always tied to his sense of national pride. I have come to learn that what unites these are the logics of racism, masculinity, and militarism: every time Mark retells a story of patriotic honor and personal self-worth, he is retelling a story in which he is inevitably either holding or shooting a gun. And most often, Mark's gun is there to protect him and his country from people who do not look or think like him, a group of enemies that includes "illegals," "communists," "liberals," and "gang bangers."

Mark fired his first gun at the age of eighteen. He was completing basic training a few weeks after graduating high school in Philadelphia. From the get-go, Mark was an exceptional shooter. And shooting gave Mark an enormous sense of fulfillment. "I wasn't sitting there pulling the trigger thinking, 'Hey, one day I'm going to kill somebody,'" Mark told me. "I was thinking, 'Hey, I'm good at this. And I'm wearing the uniform of my country so it's giving me satisfaction. I can help defend this nation if I have to.'"

A self-described "small, skinny guy," Mark says his friends laughed at him when he said he wanted to become a marine. "They were like, 'Look at you, you won't make it through.' And you know what?" he continued, "There were times where the bigger guys in the platoon were crying, and I would just lay there with a smile on my face." As he has repeatedly pointed out to me in the fifteen years that I have known him, when it came time for him to graduate, "I didn't stand with my platoon because I got high shooter. I stood with three other guys that got high shooter in their platoon and four other guys that got the physical fitness award. . . . So that was a major accomplishment for me. Here I am getting recognized. Standing with a small group of guys that stood out from the rest."

After leaving the Marine Corps shortly before the first Gulf War, Mark returned to Philadelphia, where he worked as an electrician, eventually starting his own company. He purchased his first gun shortly thereafter from a friend from the military. A few years later, through the same friend, Mark became involved in several paramilitary groups in Pennsylvania—a hodgepodge he describes as made up of "survivalists, militia guys, and people doing border operations." It was around this time that Mark began making trips to Arizona, often spending weeks at a time patrolling the border.

In 2008, at the height of the financial crisis, Mark's electrical repair company went under. Angry and in need of income, he turned to what he knew best: teaching people how to use guns.

Three years ago, Mark decided to return to Arizona. This time, it wasn't to patrol the border, it was to settle down and develop his firearms business. "Back [in the Northeast], the rules were just too strict," Mark told me. "It was too hard to start my business up there. Plus, I just got fed up with all the liberals."

In today's America, one of the best predictors of party affiliation is gun ownership. Consider the 2016 presidential election: 63 percent of voters living in gun-owning households backed Donald Trump, while 65 percent of those living in a house without a gun backed Hillary Clinton.[1] While this polarization may seem commonsensical and intuitive to us today, recent research by political scientists at the University of Kansas suggests that this has not always been the case.[2]

Analyzing data from 1972 to 2012, Mark Joslyn and his colleagues show that the political divide between gun owners and non–gun owners has grown dramatically over time. Gun owners were 50 percent more likely to vote for a Republican in 2012 than they were in 1972. This suggests two important things: First, being a gun owner is about much more than owning a gun; rather, it is a complex political identity connected to attitudes and beliefs. Second, this political identity has developed and hardened over time. Indeed, as I have come to learn in my research, for people like Mark, owning a gun is as much about identifying in opposition to something as it is to identifying with something.

The liberals—or "they," as Mark often labels people on the Left—form one of Mark's many enemies. When he was patrolling the border, he would tell me that "they" falsely accused him of racism and sexism: "They say that we're the ones who are racist, that we hate women, when meanwhile all these backwards Mexicans with their machismo culture are going around raping their women. But they don't like to talk about that." And these days he tells me that "they" falsely accuse him of being the cause of gun violence in America while overlooking the true source:

> There is no laws that could have been passed that would have stopped what the guy in Vegas did. And that's the truth. . . . Millions of, tens of millions of semiautomatics are in American hands, and in any given year about three hundred rifles are used in crimes. That's it. But I just find the hypocrisy amazing. Because now you got the Dems screaming about gun control again, but yet they don't speak about the black-on-black crime in this country. They don't scream about Chicago. The numbers in Chicago are higher than Iraq. It's ridiculous.

There are some things I do not entirely know about Mark, but one thing I can tell you for certain: Mark could care less about the violence in Chicago. Rather, just as with the pundits on Fox News and the spokespeople for pro-gun organizations across the country, he calls attention to the violence in Chicago (which in reality has a homicide rate roughly a third of that of Iraq) to try to delegitimize any conversation about gun control. His concern is not the people in Chicago whose lives are being ruined by gun violence; it's him and his access to guns. And in these views, Mark has a spokesman in Donald Trump.

When I asked Mark to explain why Trump is bad for his business he told me, "Cause nobody is scared. I make money off peoples' fear. When people are scared, that's when they want to take classes."

When Mark says that "nobody is scared" under Trump, he is thinking about people like him—conservative white men, "gun people," as he calls his tribe. Among the things that "gun people" like Mark are no longer scared of are laws regulating firearms. "Trump said from day one he was a gun guy," Mark explained. "The federal government isn't going to make gun laws, so people feel, 'Oh, I can still go out and buy this stuff whenever I want. I don't need to do a panic buy.' Like they did when Obama first got elected, and then when he got elected again."

The data suggest that Mark is right. While gun purchases have tended to spike after presidential elections, often fueled by the regulatory fears Mark referenced, there was no such spike when Trump was elected. Furthermore, although gun sales increased nearly every single month under Obama and are still higher in the United States than in any other country in the world, they have declined in all but one of the months that Trump has been in office.[3]

Gun laws make up one important element in the matrix of things Mark is no longer worried about, but there are others. For one thing, Mark is no longer worried that one of his enemies is in power. Where Obama represented danger, Trump represents safety. "Trump is up there fighting for people like me," Mark enthusiastically told me.

Just as Trump is fighting for Mark, so, too, is Mark fighting for Trump. "We had Trump here a few weeks ago," Mark told me, referring to the rally Trump held in Phoenix in August. "I was there patrolling with a few guys." In this iteration of patrolling, the enemy was not "illegals" but "communists." "We have this club out here called the John Brown Gun Club," Mark told me, referring to a local antifascist gun club named after the abolitionist who sought to initiate an armed slave revolt at Harpers Ferry in 1859. "They are communists, and you can tell they are communists because they wear the red bandanas, the same as the Khmer Rouge in Cambodia did. So some people come to these protests wearing the gear, wearing rifles. And so we were there to offer extra security in case they started something."

By complete coincidence, I happened to be writing this essay in Harpers Ferry, where I was attending a wedding. As I walked around the town I came across two memorials. The first was for John Brown and the twenty-one men who fought with him. The second was for Private Luke Quinn, a marine just like Mark, who was killed in the process of participating in a raid, led by Robert E. Lee, to capture John Brown's group. Two memorials; two divergent accounts of history.

On the one hand, the Trump administration needs to be understood as something new. On the other hand, it needs to be understood as an extension of our past ways. What Mark can teach us is the extent to which the Trump presidency represents at once a change and, importantly, a continuation of a longer history. It is a history whose pillars are racism, militarization, and working-class economic decline.

It was not Trump who waged a war on communism in the Far East but rather Lyndon Johnson and Richard Nixon. It was not Trump who launched the first war in Iraq but rather George H. W. Bush. It was not Trump who began to militarize the border and speak of illegal immigration as a national-security threat but rather Bill Clinton. And it was not Trump who helped destroy the stability of working-class employment in America but rather a long list of our presidents, not least of whom was Barack Obama.

Yes, Trump expresses stronger support for gun rights than we have heard from presidents before. But we have been on this road for many years. Mark is emblematic of a society that has long addressed its fears by turning to the militarization of everyday life.

No movement over the past fifty years has made as significant gains as the gun-rights movement. Civil rights, women's rights, gay rights—these all pale in comparison to what the gun-rights movement has accomplished. From "shall-issue" laws, which make it much easier for a person to obtain a license to carry a concealed handgun with them nearly everywhere they go, to stand-your-ground laws, which make it much easier for a person to legally kill someone, to more recent legislation like "campus carry" laws, which allow people to bring guns into the classrooms of college campuses, the past few decades have witnessed the steady proliferation not only guns of in American society but also of laws and ideas that support the ability of people like Mark to access, carry, and use those guns.

In some ways both Mark and America have changed over the past fifteen years. But in many ways both have merely extended their former ways. Fifteen years ago, Mark was in Arizona arming himself against "illegals" and al-Qaeda; today he is there arming himself against Antifa and ISIS.

Antifa said November 4 is when they are starting the civil war. Did you hear about this? In LA or Chicago, I can't remember. About twelve of them were on a highway holding up signs that said, "Nov 4th It Begins." And they are calling for violence. Antifa already claimed that the Vegas shooter was one of theirs so that

> they could take out Trump supporters. And ISIS claimed this guy
> as one of theirs. So I'm part of a team that's going to be monitor-
> ing Antifa out here come November 4.

"Antifa claimed that the Vegas shooter was one of theirs." "ISIS claimed he was one of theirs." And, just moments before making these contradictory and, in part, false declarations, Mark told me he was certain the Vegas shooter was "mentally ill . . . and proba-bly on some kinds of drugs." What do we do with these inconsis-tent statements? How are we to make sense of the fact that, on the one hand, Mark says that people like him feel less scared today than ever before while, on the other hand, they walk around armed and speak about a new set of dangers—Antifa, ISIS, the John Brown Gun Club?

I am, frankly, unsure as to whether Mark truly believes all of what he says about the Las Vegas shooter. But what I am certain about is that these ideas, which circulate in the social and politi-cal communities he traverses, matter to Mark because they are working in the service of his identity—his identity as an armed American. Mark needs to think the world is dangerous because he needs his gun, not the other way around. Indeed, the foundation of Mark's identity, from the age of eighteen, when he fired that first gun and received accolades for his marksmanship, is not the establishment of a secure America but rather an insecure one.

It has gotten to the point where Mark cannot even imagine what the world would look like without his sense of insecurity. And in this, Mark is not alone. Unfortunately, it seems that in the current political moment, Donald Trump is driving us further and further into identities that emerge not through consensus but through opposition, not in the interest of working toward establishing safety but rather in producing danger.

NOTES

1. Nate Cohn and Kevin Quealy, "Nothing Divides Voters Like Owning a Gun," *New York Times*, October 5, 2017, https://www.nytimes.com/interactive/2017/10/05/upshot/gun-ownership-partisan-divide.html.

2. Mark R. Joslyn, Donald P. Haider-Markel, Michael Baggs, and Andrew Bilbo, "Emerging Political Identities? Gun Ownership and Voting in Presidential Elections," *Social Science Quarterly* 98, no. 2 (2017): 382–96.

3. Sy Mukherjee, "Why Donald Trump Is Bad for Gun Sales," *Fortune*, September 11, 2017, http://fortune.com/2017/09/11/trump-gun-sales-decline/. See also David Sherfinski, "Under Trump, Gun Sales Fall Dramatically," *Washington Times*, August 8, 2017, http://www.washingtontimes.com/news/2017/aug/8/under-donald-trump-gun-sales-fall-dramatically/.

BLACK WOMEN AND THE FBI

ASHLEY FARMER

According to a recently leaked FBI report, the agency is now watching a new group they have labeled "Black Identity Extremists." These "BIE" groups, the Bureau asserts, are motivated by "perceptions of police brutality against African Americans" and have "spurred an increase in premeditated, retaliatory lethal violence against law enforcement." The FBI's renewed targeting of black activists coincides with the Trump administration's efforts to label minorities—Mexicans, Muslims, and African Americans—as potential national-security threats. The recent report should not come as a surprise. For more than a century, the American government has surveilled and harassed activists from marginalized communities. However, organizers from these marginalized communities have also established a long tradition of resisting this suppression.

No surveillance program is more intertwined with the federal government than the Counterintelligence Program (COINTELPRO). Headed by FBI director J. Edgar Hoover, COINTELPRO began in 1956 to track and disrupt the activities of the Communist Party. The program expanded significantly in the 1960s, aiming to, in Hoover's words, "expose, disrupt, misdirect, discredit, or otherwise neutralize the activities" of a range of moderate, progressive, and radical groups.[1] The federal government sanctioned decades-long surveillance of a wide range of activists, including Dr. Martin Luther King Jr., Malcolm X, and groups like the Black Panther Party and the National Association for the Advancement of Colored People (NAACP).

At Hoover's behest, a legion of special agents wiretapped organizers' homes; followed their families and harassed them with menacing phone calls that threatened to expose family secrets; posed as activists and infiltrated organizations; and raided the offices and homes of activists—all actions that periodically led to agents killing those targeted men and women.

The male victims of such surveillance have gotten the lion's share of attention over the years. Yet many women, too, were targeted. Their stories of resistance are important not just as historical footnotes but also in helping today's generation of activists as they struggle to navigate the increasingly perilous currents of our moment.

In the 1950s, the Bureau hounded women organizers whom they deemed to be "subversives" and "communists." Most of the women whom they targeted, however, were simply local-level activists engaged in labor and civil-rights organizing within progressive groups. As COINTELPRO expanded, so, too, did Hoover's tracking of black women. By the 1960s, this intensified, with special agents surveilling black women activists who led welfare-rights organizations, those who engaged in voter-registration work through the NAACP and the Student Nonviolent Coordinating Committee (SNCC), as well as more radical groups like the Black Panther Party. The FBI's ever-growing list of "threats" included activists ranging from the black-nationalist "Queen Mother" Audley Moore to the NAACP and SNCC leader Ella Baker to novelists and the poets Pauli Murray and Sonia Sanchez, among many others.

The Bureau used a network made up largely of white men, so-called special agents, to monitor black women activists. Surveillance could mean a special agent walking ten steps behind as activists strolled in the park with their children. It could materialize as an unfamiliar face in a community meeting. It could resemble a friendly neighbor who asked a few too many questions. Despite the harassment, these black women labored, organized, and survived, developing multifaceted strategies for challenging surveillance.

A central goal of the Bureau was to identify and isolate social-justice activists in order to scare them into submission and silence. In response, many activists directly confronted the FBI. Some women, like Audley Moore, volunteered for questioning. Moore was a lifelong radical activist, with ties to major progressive and radical organizations throughout the sixty years spanning the 1930s to the 1990s. During the Great Depression, she organized black workers to fight for economic justice. In the 1940s and 1950s, she supported black soldiers and veterans, as well as poor and working-class black women victimized by the state. By the 1960s, she was considered a seasoned organizer and mentored younger activists, including members of the Black Panther Party.

Moore's indispensable role in social-justice organizing drew Hoover's ire. The FBI surveilled her from the 1930s until the 1980s. As the Bureau performed its interrogations, Moore let them know that they, too, were under scrutiny. When they brought her in for interrogation, she turned their inquiries back on them. She questioned the FBI agents about their suppression tactics and rebuked their racism. "Without being asked," the agents noted, she confirmed that she was a member of multiple radical organizations and remarked that she "had noticed nothing but White men" in the building, arguing that they must not hire black agents. Moore ended the interview by asserting her resistance to oppression, stating that "she would not be a witness" against other activists in court and that "she did not wish to be interviewed again."

Artists such as poet Nikki Giovanni publicized the FBI's surveillance in their craft. In her 1968 poem "A Short Essay of Affirmation Explaining Why (With Apologies to the Federal Bureau of Investigation)," Giovanni pinpointed the Bureau's tactics, how they placed "That little microphone / In our teeth / Between our thighs / Or anyplace." The Bureau's insidious techniques gave rise to black activists' pervasive and well-founded paranoia about spying and infiltration. Giovanni defended those shaken by the Bureau's ubiquitous infiltrations, noting that those activists who seemed like they talked "to themselves" were really responding to surveillance or "kn[ew] who [they were] talking to."[2]

Black women activists also banded together to combat the Bureau's dogged pursuit of their families. They created networks to help care for children, thwart intelligence gathering, and provide financial support when they and their families lost their jobs and homes and when their children were expelled from school. Some women moved in together or closer to one another to help share the burden of raising and protecting their children. Others met regularly to discuss politics and practical ways to survive, including tactics for evading their FBI details, strategies for passing notes to friends and family members who had gone underground, and the formation of defense committees to help ease the financial strain on families under surveillance.

These networks also functioned as the organizers' own forms of intelligence. While defending their families, they shared organizing information, conferred with one another about how to strategize in legal cases against the Bureau, and discussed their personal struggles of surviving state oppression. Such relationships were a key part of their resistance to authoritarianism and helped abate the often-overlooked personal effects of state surveillance.

Organizers who were members of what the FBI deemed "black hate groups" often wound up behind bars. In the 1960s and 1970s, the government jailed them, oftentimes on trumped-up charges of everything from their membership in allegedly subversive organizations to supposedly supplying arms for violent confrontations to kidnapping. These activists, including Mae Mallory, Angela Davis, Ericka Huggins, and many others, represented some of the Bureau's most high-profile attempts to jail black thinkers and organizers based on false claims about "premeditated, retaliatory lethal violence against law enforcement," the same charges being levied against so-called Black Identity Extremists today.

The imprisoned activists and intellectuals challenged the surveillance state through writing. They developed a vibrant body of literature that spanned regions, organizational affiliations, and political orientations and that documented the mental, physical, and psychological abuse they endured as COINTELPRO targets. They also used their intellectual production to expose the multilayered logic of state persecution, connecting the federal government's surveillance tactics to state police forces' subversion of legal codes to local jail wardens' violations of their civil liberties.

Whether it was Huggins's poetry about her experiences as a political prisoner, Mallory's prison letters warning black organizers about FBI and State Department tactics, or Davis's searing analyses of the inner workings of state-sanctioned surveillance and imprisonment, black women organizers produced publications aimed at addressing the intersectional and insidious reach of and potential resistance to surveillance. Such intimate knowledge of authoritarianism gave these black women the material to theorize about how to mobilize against oppression. Their publications offer critical roadmaps to the groups who have already been or will soon be labeled as subversive organizations.

The current FBI's labeling of activist groups as "extremists" signals the depth and reach of surveillance and suppression that we are likely to endure during this administration. To survive, we will need to rely on the knowledge of those who are intimately familiar with these practices. Black women activists from Moore to Giovanni, Huggins to Davis, have offered a multifaceted program of action. They have shown us that we must consistently and publicly expose the government's tactics. We must also close ranks around those who are drawing government fire by offering financial and emotional support. Finally, we must create an intersectional coalition to fight this oppression.

Drawing on their own experiences, black women organizers offer us theories of resistance that encompass organizers' personal and political lives. We can be inspired by their courage and rely on their knowledge at this moment when the surveillance systems of the state have, once more, placed progressive and radical activists firmly in their sights.

NOTES

1. J. Edgar Hoover, memorandum to all FBI offices on "Counter Intelligence Program, Black Nationalist—Hate Groups, Internal Security," August 25, 1967.
2. Nikki Giovanni, *The Collected Poetry of Nikki Giovanni* (New York: Harper-Collins, 2008), 21.

CONFEDERATE REVISIONIST HISTORY

DOUGLAS S. MASSEY

Donald Trump was elected on a wave of unrestrained white nationalism that promised to "take back our country" and in so doing "make America great again." His pandering to white racial resentment throughout the campaign was open and unapologetic. To whites who felt that their social status had been reduced by the advances in racial equity achieved through decades of Civil Rights struggles; to those whom Republicans since Richard Nixon's "southern strategy" had pandered to with so-called dogwhistle politics; to those who could not reconcile themselves to Obama's election as president—that is, to the election of an African American to the nation's highest office—Trump spoke their language of racial fury and overt prejudice.

It therefore came as no surprise when, as president, he defended the white nationalists who marched in Charlottesville as including "some very fine people" and expressed his support for "those people [who] were there to protest the taking down of the statue of Robert E. Lee," whom he equated with founding fathers such as George Washington and Thomas Jefferson. More recently, the White House chief of staff called Robert E. Lee "an honorable man" and stated that "the lack of an ability to compromise led to the Civil

War, and men and women of good faith on both sides made their stand."

The controversy over the removal of Confederate monuments offers an opportunity to counter one of the biggest lies in American public discourse: the view that the Civil War was fought over the issue of "states' rights" rather than slavery. It is common for whites in both the North and the South to argue that the Stars and Bars and Confederate monuments are symbols of "heritage, not hate." In their telling, the Confederate rebellion was not about slavery and white supremacy but instead an honorable attempt to stop a despotic federal government from abridging the rights of states guaranteed under the U.S. Constitution.

Nothing could be further from the truth, and if Americans are ever to progress in eradicating the stain of racism, they must acknowledge that the Confederacy was not—never was and never could become—a noble cause. Although in defeat Southerners invented the myth that the Civil War was fought to preserve "states' rights," this rationalization was an ex post facto whitewash of the truth. In reality, the Confederacy was simply a treasonous revolt undertaken in defense of slavery. At the time of secession, the U.S. Constitution did not prohibit slavery. Indeed, Southern delegates to the Constitutional Convention of 1787 had made quite sure that slavery would be preserved and protected in the original constitutional order.

Six slave states and six free states sent delegations to the convention in Philadelphia (Rhode Island did not send any delegates). Each state was given one vote and nine votes were required to pass any measure, thus giving the southern states effective veto power in drafting the constitution. In addition, twenty-five of the convention's fifty-five delegates were themselves slave holders, with a huge self-interest in preserving slavery. Of the eighty-four clauses in the original constitution, six concerned slaves and their owners, and five had implications for slavery. And of these eleven clauses, ten protected the institution of chattel slavery.

Although the clauses and their implications for slavery were openly debated, the framers were nonetheless shamefaced about the fact that the new constitution, ostensibly drafted to "secure the blessings of liberty," in fact authorized the enslavement of 18 percent of the new nation's inhabitants. Adopting what historians have called the "principle of nondisclosure," the words slave and slavery were deliberately stricken from the original document, along with any mention of Africans or Negroes. In the original Constitution, slaves simply became persons "held to Service or Labour," or simply "other Persons."

Southern delegates used their veto power not just to preserve slavery's existence at the time of the Constitution's writing and ratification but to render it impossible ever to eliminate slavery subsequently through constitutional means. Proposed amendments to the constitution required approval by two-thirds of both houses of Congress or two-thirds of all states, and to bolster the legislative power of the South, each state was given two senators regardless of population size. And slaves were counted as three-fifths of a person for purposes of apportionment, even though they couldn't vote. And if a proposed amendment somehow did manage to achieve the required a two-thirds majority in each chamber, ratification itself required approval by three-quarters of state legislatures. With six slave states and seven free states at the time of the Constitution's adoption, the passage of an amendment to abolish slavery was thus inconceivable to the founders.

As time passed, however, territorial expansion created the possibility of many more than thirteen states, and each additional state added to the union necessarily threatened the balance of power between slave and free states. With the 1803 Louisiana Purchase, the 1846 Oregon Treaty, and the 1848 Treaty of Guadalupe

Hidalgo, the United States came to span the entire continent. Although the Missouri Compromise evaded conflict for a time by informally agreeing not to admit new slave states above the line that ran east-west through Missouri's southern border, during the 1850s there were vicious battles—prologues to the war that followed—fought over whether territories such as Kansas were to be admitted as free or slave states.

The Confederate rebellion of 1861 did not stem from any direct threat to abolish slavery. Rather, it was a response to the new Republican Party's platform, which simply proposed that no additional slave states be admitted to the union. Such a policy created the possibility that at some point in the distant future, free states *might* approach the three-quarters needed to amend the Constitution and *possibly* seek to abolish slavery. It was this remote possibility that drove Southern states to rebellion, not any immediate threat by federal authorities to overturn slavery in the states where it then existed. Indeed, in the run-up to Fort Sumter, President Lincoln made it quite clear that he was willing to compromise on the issue of slavery's extension in order to preserve the union.

Thus, the Confederate revolt was not about states' rights; it was about protecting the institution of chattel slavery from a remote future threat. Proof of the centrality of slavery to the Southern cause lies in the Confederate Constitution itself, in which the cryptic references to persons "held to Service or Labour" were replaced with explicit references to slaves and Negroes. Article 1, section 9, paragraph 3, for example, stated that "no bill of attainder, ex post facto law, or law denying or impairing the right of property in *negro slaves* shall be passed" (italics my own). Apart from these substitutions, the Confederate Constitution was identical to the original U.S. Constitution in all respects.

The true purpose of the Southern rebellion was clearly articulated by the Confederate vice president Alexander Stephens in his

"Cornerstone" speech, delivered on March 21, 1861, in Savannah, Georgia. In it, he assured the crowd of white secessionists that "the new constitution has put at rest, forever, all the agitating questions relating to our peculiar institution—African slavery as it exists amongst us—the proper status of the Negro in our form of civilization. This was the immediate cause of the late rupture and present revolution." Indeed, he went on to state that the new constitution's "cornerstone rests upon the great truth, that the Negro is not equal to the white man; that slavery—subordination to the superior race—is his natural and normal condition."

As a graduate of West Point and an officer in the United States Army, Robert E. Lee had, of course, sworn to protect and defend the Constitution of the United States. As we have seen, however, the Republican Party platform posed no threat to the constitution and was in no way a violation of its provisions. It simply articulated a principled stand against the spread of slavery and did not call for abolition in the states where it then existed. The truth is that Lee chose to protect and defend slavery and not the Constitution to which he had pledged his allegiance, an act that can only be defined as treason, and so it was for all those who joined him in revolt.

The idea that the Civil War was fought to preserve states' rights was a postwar fabrication invented by defeated Confederates to elide the fact that their bloody sacrifices had not only been in vain but their blood had been spilled for an ignoble cause. The only states' right that Southerners *ever* really cared about was the right to subjugate and exploit black people. Before the Civil War, when Northern states passed laws granting the protections of citizenship to runaway slaves within their jurisdictions, they adamantly opposed *that* states' right.

White Northerners, of course, are not blameless when it comes to the perpetuation of racial inequality in the United States. Indeed, after the Civil War they were complicit in acquiescing to the myth of states' rights. Although Northerners initially took vigorous actions to enforce black civil rights throughout the South, when Southerners responded with an unceasing campaign of terrorism and guerilla warfare the Northern political classes ultimately grew tired of the effort, and after 1876 abandoned Reconstruction. In so doing, they left African Americans to their fate at the hands of former Confederates.

From that point onward, whites outside the South ceased to challenge the states'-rights narrative and turned a blind eye to the creation of a new system of racial subordination. Blithely ignoring the endemic discrimination and violence perpetrated on African Americans in the South, whites increasingly focused their attention on the business of prospering in the nation's new industrial economy. As black out-migration from the South accelerated in the twentieth century, racial attitudes hardened in the North and West as well; through housing ordinances, redlining, and other methods, Northerners built their own de facto system of racial segregation and exclusion.

Donald Trump's defense of white nationalists and their efforts to prevent the removal of Confederate monuments provides an opening finally to tell the truth about the Southern rebellion. The time has come to challenge the myth of states' rights promulgated today by neo-Confederates and their sympathizers throughout the nation. Assertions that symbols of the Confederacy somehow represent a proud "Southern heritage" or symbolize the resistance of freedom-loving states to the oppressive predations of a too-powerful federal government must be categorically and publicly rejected.

The United States never had the benefit of a truth commission in the wake of the Civil War, nor was there ever any formal accounting for the systematic violence done to African Americans during Reconstruction and under Jim Crow. For years, in polite discussions whites simply have "agreed to disagree" about the real causes of the Confederate revolt and averted their gaze from the system of racial injustice that replaced slavery. It is thus imperative at this time that Donald Trump and the white nationalists who support him be directly and openly challenged in their claim that Confederate symbols represent heritage and not hate and that the Civil War was fought over states' rights rather than slavery.

The plain truth is that the Confederate states launched an unconstitutional armed insurrection against the legitimate government of the United States that resulted in the death of more than 700,000 Americans, more than in all other American wars combined. A revolt to preserve slavery is not something Americans should honor with stately monuments or florid displays of the Confederate Battle Flag. In reality, these symbols are tokens of a bloody war fought in defense of a dehumanizing institution, whose only purpose was to enrich a class of wealthy property owners while giving otherwise oppressed poor white Southerners someone even lower on the totem pole to look down upon. It is not a pretty picture.

NOTE

Revised May 25, 2018.

TRUMP'S CHARISMA

STEVEN LUKES

Accepting the presidential nomination at the 2016 Republican convention, Donald Trump painted a picture of America in crisis, with "poverty and violence at home" and "war and destruction abroad." But, he proclaimed, "I am your voice" and "I alone can fix it." The fired-up delegates, booing on cue and cheering when prompted, roared in response with chants of "USA!" "Lock her up!" "Build the wall!" and "Trump! Trump! Trump!" Was this the power of charisma? And how long will it last?

It was Max Weber who imported the concept of charisma from its religious meaning of a divinely conferred gift into the sociology of political power. It has since entered everyday vocabulary, as *Merriam-Webster* reports: first, that of everyday political commentary, to mean "a personal magic of leadership arousing special popular loyalty or enthusiasm for a public figure (such as a political leader)," and then, even more widely and vaguely, to signify "a special magnetic charm or appeal," as in "the *charisma* of a popular actor."

If we want to explore its relevance to the present moment, it will best to return to Weber's usage. His "charisma" brought together a number of features of a particular form of what Weber called *Herrschaft*—the power to compel people to obey. It differs sharply from two other forms: the "traditional" (where people obey because of age-old laws and customs) and the "rational-legal" (whose authority comes from widely accepted impersonal and impartial rules). These two forms sustain the everyday (*alltäglich*) order and routines of traditional and bureaucratic life. They contribute to continuity and permanence. Weber saw such order as an essential background for economic growth under capitalism.

Charisma, by contrast, is exceptional and disruptive. It is "specifically extraordinary" (*spezifisch ausseralltäglich*). It is in the first place, he wrote, highly *personal*. It is a "certain quality of an individual personality, by virtue of which he is set apart from ordinary men and treated as endowed with supernatural, superhuman, or at least specifically extraordinary power or qualities." These are "not accessible to the ordinary person, but are regarded as of divine origin or as exemplary, and on the basis of them, the individual concerned is treated as a leader." The social relations involved are "purely personal": the followers have an entirely personal devotion to the leader and this is elicited by, in the words of Christopher Adair-Toteff, "the 'leader's' ability to seem to be able to perform 'miracles' or to perform heroic acts." [1] They recognize the personal qualifications and characteristics of the charismatic leader, whom they view as having been chosen, as belonging to God's grace. The religious analogies are significant. Charisma is linked by Weber with both magic and prophecy, realms where power derives from personal gifts.

And yet, as Weber makes clear, the power is only effective insofar as it is seen to be. The charismatic leader depends on his followers for recognition. Once the followers cease to believe in the leader, the leader's charismatic power disappears. So charisma, second, requires *perpetual reanimation*. And third, Weber thought, it is *temporary* because, like magic, its appeal and its efficacy only last as long as it is seen to be successful. The charismatic leader,

Weber wrote, is "the eternally new" and is fated to descend from a "stormy and emotional" beginning to a "slow suffocating death under the weight of material interests." The emotional bonding resulting from excessive expectations will not long survive the perceived failure to fulfill them.

Charisma is, fourth, *irrational*. Like the mystic, the charismatic leader is believed in because his message goes against common knowledge of how the world works, because it rejects and disrupts what is taken for granted, including the everyday pursuit of interests and the impersonal norms governing daily life. Weber thought that this meant that pure charisma rejects economic gain and indeed any type of routine and regulated economic life. (But, as we know, many charismatic leaders have, for a time, been seen as economic saviors: Hitler put Germany back to work and ended hyperinflation, and under Mussolini, as the saying goes, the trains ran on time.)

Finally, we should note that Weber, as social scientist, sought to leave charisma's moral worth an open question. In fact, he was himself ambivalent about charismatic leadership in politics. Aware of the dangers of demagoguery, he nonetheless valued the role of passion in politics and admired leaders like Pericles, who could display greatness and inspire their followers. Charismatic leaders could resist the ever-growing disenchantment of a graying world that was under the increasing sway of soulless experts and bureaucrats. On the other hand, he also wrote of the charismatic leader as a "demonic" type who appears only in chaotic times. Scholars and commentators have seen historical and contemporary leaders as charismatic in Weber's sense. Weber himself mentioned Cleon and Napoleon. Hitler, Mussolini, Churchill, and Gandhi are often described as charismatic, and Raymond Aron thought that de Gaulle was the perfect embodiment of Weberian charisma.

What, then, a year and a half into his presidency, are we to say concerning Donald Trump? Before going any further we should note that what Weber gives us is a sketch, a caricature. What he called a pure "ideal type" is abstracted from real cases in which, to get their way, political leaders draw on multiple sources of power: the threat of force, tradition, legal authority, economic muscle, incentives, negotiating skill, coalitional alliances, and so on, with more or less success. So our question should be: to what extent has Trump's exercising of presidential power approximated Weber's ideal-typical picture of how charisma works?

The answer is: remarkably closely. He has not shown himself to be adept at using the various sources of power just indicated; least of all has he been successful at political deal-making. But he has succeeded at being exceptional and disruptive. Just compare him—his persona and demeanor—with the sixteen Republican presidential contenders, whom he felled like ninepins (and with most previous Republican presidents and the current vice president) and who are all what Weber would have called *alltäglich*—everyday, ordinary, and order-sustaining. Indeed, by historical standards, those defeated candidates are unusually so: remarkably mediocre, small-minded, and narrowly focused.

In office, Trump has disdained Weber's other two forms of power, which are both order preserving: traditional and legal-rational. He has bypassed and subverted presidential traditions. As a president he is unprecedented, in numerous ways. He has refused to release his taxes, retained his lucrative business interests, communicated to the people via tweets, run White House business chaotically, installed his family into the administration, surrounded himself with generals, exhibited systematic hostility to and contempt for the press, rejected compromises with political opposition, brought far-right forces into the mainstream, contributed hugely to the coarsening of public discourse, and, in sum, adopted the advice of his former chief strategist Steve Bannon to "deconstruct the administrative state."

Bannon's grandiose project (inspired, apparently, by Lenin) is also, of course, nothing less than the deconstruction of legal-rational authority, of which we have seen some significant instances. Thus, Trump's appointments to head administrative agencies have been directly subversive of their functions: he has, rather systematically, selected persons who are either opposed to the agencies' missions or have violated the laws they are meant to implement, and he has left many other important leadership positions unfilled. When it suits him, he attacks his own Department of Justice and intelligence services. And he has revealed his, shall we say, "flexible" attitude toward impersonal and impartial application of laws by pardoning a sheriff who was found guilty of doing exactly the opposite; by his encouragement of rough treatment of suspects by the police; and by his repeated attempts, so far unsuccessful, to obstruct the investigation of Russian tampering with his election.

Charisma, Weber insisted, is inherently personal. Given the public's longstanding familiarity with Trump as a TV celebrity and given the extravagant narcissism of his personality, when applied to him, the term already seems drastically understated. Add to all this his astonishingly hubristic claim that "I alone can fix it," regarding Middle Eastern terrorism and a host of other issues, and you have a clear instance of what a twenty-first-century cult of personality looks like.

So far, the call has been answered with what looks like devotion from a sturdy 35 percent of the electorate. But it does need to be continually renewed, hence the singularly unpresidential ongoing resort to deliberately divisive campaign rallies. But how long can such "collective effervescences" keep the flame of devotion burning, if the promised successes cease to materialize or, perhaps more to the point, are explicitly *seen* to cease by his fan base?

Which brings us to Weber's linking of charisma to irrationality. Here Weber's considerable powers of prophecy were insufficient. For he believed that the modern world was becoming more and more rational across all spheres of life—though punctuated by charismatic interludes, some chaotic, even demonic—a process in which experts of all kinds played an ever more central role. It was beyond his imagining (and not only his) that the government and administration of a major state—of the most powerful state in the world—would succumb to the leadership of a charismatic figure for whom the very norms of rationality are, in key respects, irrelevant. To begin to take the measure of this development, we need to turn to another concept—*bullshit*—and another thinker, the philosopher Henry Frankfurt, for whom "the essence of bullshit" is "lack of connection to a concern with truth."

For the bullshitter, unlike the liar, "the truth-values of his statements are of no central interest"; he is "unconcerned with how the things about which he speaks truly are." The liar intends to deceive us about what is true; the bullshitter does not care. Many make much of President Trump's lies, but we need to grasp the significance of his bullshitting. Lying, after all, is as ancient as politics itself, but leading a multitude who follow you in discarding any concern with truth and truthfulness is something else. With policy making increasingly disconnected from expert knowledge and administrative experience, this has brought a new level of uncertainty into our politics, one that is all the more dangerous as the globe warms.

Can we then, following Weber, foresee a descent from the "stormy and emotional" beginning of the early Trump presidency to its "slow suffocating death under the weight of material interests"? There is no good reason to think that a Republican administration under Trump will advance the material interests of that portion of his followers who hope for jobs and industrial renewal rather than those of the most advantaged, who expect deregulation, a booming stock market, and lower taxes.

We can always speculate about how and when lack of success with either group will lead to the withdrawal of the recognition by which charisma lives and dies. But we also need to consider the possibility that for a significant number of core followers and supporters it may not—that their material interests will not weigh heavily enough with them to be decisive. Perhaps the charismatic power of the bigoted successor to the United States' first black president, a man who bans refugees, breaks up their families, and impounds their children and who wants to build a wall against immigrants, rests on other foundations.

Usually the successes attributed to charismatic leaders by their followers have been multiple: not just material, economic advancement but also the symbolic rewards of status and the assurance of being part of an imagined community. Most commentators agree that Trump's base of support is a white working class that has lost out from globalization and that looks to him with the misplaced hope that he can restore the economic basis, the jobs, and opportunities of the world they have lost.

In fact, his base extends across the country and across social classes, but the common denominator is that it is predominantly white, and it is his appeal to "whiteness" that seems to underlie his charismatic appeal. Overt racism and nationalism are once again central in American political life as more moderate Republican politicians resort to racism and nationalism to avoid being ousted from the right in primaries, often in gerrymandered constituencies. Thus, the antidiversity sentiment behind many of Trump's signature slogans—Make America Great Again, Build the Wall—has become part of the Republican Party's brand.

In this way, we are witnessing what Weber called the "routinization of charisma"—where the leader's message becomes normalized by shaping traditions and acquiring bureaucratic form, and thus Trumpism will, in many respects, survive the man himself. The longer Trump's personal charismatic connection with his followers lasts, the more likely it is that Trumpism as a movement will plant deep roots. Therefore, our most urgent priority is undermining his appeal to voters before the 2018 congressional elections: through showing Trump to be the conman that he is; through exposing the hollowness of his claims to be helping the working poor; through proposing better, more inclusive alternative policies.

For his hard-core followers, the charismatic bond may well be, as Trump has boasted, unbreakable. For the rest, who support him with varying degrees of unease, it is vital to do everything possible to help it grow: to expose his racism relentlessly, to counter the symbolic value of whiteness—the long-term hegemony of which is, in any case, demographically doomed—to offer policies that counteract the fears and insecurities from which it derives and to develop better communal narratives. Only then will there be a chance to put the brakes on America's disastrous experiment with authoritarian charismatic governance.

NOTES

Revised June 21, 2018.

1. Christopher Adair-Toteff, *Max Weber's Sociology of Religion* (Tubingen: Mohr Siebeck, 2016), 36.

UNEQUAL AMERICA

MICHELLE JACKSON AND DAVID B. GRUSKY

The United States was once widely—and quite uncynically—viewed as a land of prosperity and opportunity. During the expansionary decades of the mid-twentieth century, it was treated as the world's test case on the matter of whether capitalism, once properly tamed, could deliver prosperity and opportunity for all. Although no one imagined that the taming of capitalism would be easy or straightforward, there was at least widespread hope that the United States could ultimately deliver the middle-class dream to many.

This benign vision of the future now seems rather quaint and has given way to various dystopian alternatives. What happened to old-fashioned American hopefulness? The simple answer: it's hard to maintain hope when loss and decline are everywhere around us.[1]

This loss takes many forms. It is experienced by children as a dramatic decline in their chances of achieving a standard of living as high as that of their parents.[2] It is experienced by men as a substantial deterioration in their earnings relative to women.[3] It is experienced by manufacturing workers as a sharp loss in the number of high-paying union jobs.[4] It is experienced by "rust belt" families as a sudden loss of employment and earnings to China and other countries.[5]

We have become—in short—a land in which economic loss and decline are omnipresent. Although many workers continue to do well, most everyone hears stories of loss in the media or has children, parents, friends, or neighbors who have experienced loss.

How do we reconcile ourselves to loss? There are two characteristic reactions: we can turn inward and blame ourselves or look outward and blame others. It has long been thought that the first response, the self-blaming one, would become dominant among those in the United States who aren't faring well. In a classic satirical essay, the British sociologist Michael Young argued that those who lose out in a merit-based economy will have no choice but to blame themselves as they will view the economy as a fair arbiter that delivers failure only to those lacking in talent or effort.[6] It is, as Young put it, "hard indeed in a society that makes so much of merit to be judged as having none."[7] We are of course now seeing much of this expected self-blaming and inward-turning behavior in the form of drug addiction, depression, and even suicide among populations that have been hit hard by loss.[8]

As Young argued, the self-blaming response should dominate in a society, like the United States, that is presumed to dispense rewards and failure fairly. It is perhaps surprising in this context that the second characteristic response to loss, the externalizing and other-blaming one, has also become very popular in the United States. It is *not* the case, in other words, that those who are losing out are necessarily blaming themselves. Instead, they're often blaming others who are seen as benefiting unjustly from policies that, although initially established to rectify injustice, have now in fact "gone too far." The contemporary populist response doesn't, then, stem from the view that our reform efforts have fallen short but from the view that they've gone too far.

It is not always appreciated how widespread this externalizing view is. In the United States, a full 43 percent of adults claim that "discrimination against whites has become as big a problem as discrimination against blacks and other minorities," and as many as 60 percent of white working-class adults make the same claim.[9]

The same externalizing response shows up in recent ethnographic research. In her already-classic study of working-class whites in Louisiana, Arlie Hochschild shows that they subscribe to a "deep story" representing affirmative action, antidiscrimination law, and antipoverty programs as illicit sources of advantage for African Americans and immigrants.[10] These various initiatives to rectify historic disadvantage are now represented as "overshooting the mark" and generating unfair losses among those who have long been advantaged. In this way, losses have been turned into grievances, albeit ones that rely on a misguided assessment of the extent to which government programs have reduced illicit inequalities.

The same narrative underlies populist objections to initiatives addressing gender discrimination and other gender-based inequalities. As but one recent example, a Google employee internally circulated a ten-page manifesto emphasizing the biological sources of gender inequality, replete with warnings that Google's regulatory overreach is "unfair, divisive, and bad for business."[11]

This "overcorrecting" metaphor even underlies populist objections to protrade regulation. The standard argument here is that the mounting deficit, rather than being attributable to fair and open competition, has been driven by unfair and uncompetitive rules that overcorrect for historical trade barriers and prevent the United States from competing on fair terms. This position was adopted, for example, in Donald Trump's campaign criticisms of "China's outrageous theft of intellectual property, along with their illegal product dumping and their devastating currency manipulation."[12] It also appears in one of his early executive orders directing the Commerce Department to assess whether the country's trade partners engage in "unfair and discriminatory trade practices," such as nontariff barriers, product dumping, and intellectual-property theft.[13] And it of course appears in his recent threats to place stiff tariffs on as much as $200B of imports from China.

The resulting populist project thus has far more intellectual coherence than is sometimes appreciated. It proceeds from the consistently voiced view that historically disadvantaged groups and countries (e.g., African Americans, women, China) have unfairly benefited from new legal protections and regulations. These initiatives are represented time and again as overshooting the mark and providing unfair advantage to formerly disadvantaged groups.

The skeptic might suggest that we are overstating the case. It might be argued that contemporary grievances are more directly rooted in simple racial, gender, or nativist animus than some intellectual rationalization to the effect that equalizing initiatives have "overcorrected." There is of course no denying the role of animus. But an animus-only argument fails to acknowledge that animus gains power when it's wrapped in a sacred principle.

The sacred principle in this case is a commitment to restoring fair and open competition and allowing talent to carry the day. If one believes, as most U.S. populists do, that whites, natives, and men are intrinsically more talented and productive, then their losses become prima facie evidence that recent initiatives have overcorrected and prevented true merit from prevailing. It follows from this logic that, by restoring fair and open competition, the intrinsic merit of whites, natives, and men will be properly revealed and again generate the higher pay and employment rates of the past.

This rhetoric matters deeply because it allows underlying animus to be recast as an all-American commitment to fair competition. It is neatly packaged in a seductive story about overly aggressive reform efforts providing unmerited advantage to disadvantaged groups. According to *Breitbart* journalist James Pinkerton, the populists are in this sense just like the Silent Majority of the late 1960s, as both groups appeal to "the tenets of the American Dream" and feel that they've been "taken advantage of by others, mostly on the left."[14]

The resulting populist backlash generates mutually exclusive groups locked in a zero-sum contest for resources and economic well-being. The very same losses that are viewed by one group as the result of regulatory overreach are viewed by the other as a wholly legitimate reduction in illicit privilege. The contest is energized precisely because each side has its principles.

This is surely not the "end of ideology" that Daniel Bell promised or the "end of history" that Francis Fukuyama described. And neither is it the individualized, unstructured, and nonconflictual society that other social commentators of the 1950s and 1960s envisaged. We are instead witnessing the beginning of a new era in which sharply defined groups have deeply felt grievances founded on coherent ideologies.

Is there a way forward? It might be thought that the only solution is to pull back on those various equalizing reforms that have closed intergroup gaps in pay, employment, and other outcomes. The standard case for pulling back is that, blinded by our reformist zeal, we have forgotten that those who lose out will not go quietly and will instead actively support populist movements that then undermine further reform. The only way to avoid triggering this populist reaction, so it's argued, is to more carefully mete out reform.

This "go-slow" argument, typically marketed as properly pragmatic, is in fact highly unrealistic. Its key problem is that it's impossible to defend a go-slow approach when discrimination and other illicit sources of inequality remain so profoundly large. Because it's impossible to justify going slow, we cannot expect that women, immigrants, African Americans, and other long-disadvantaged groups will stand down merely because their more advantaged counterparts have become activated. It seems more likely that such resistance will only induce disadvantaged groups to redouble their efforts.

If going slow won't work, is there some other way out? There is. It entails recognizing that intergroup comparisons become less pronounced when economic growth is widely shared. This approach doesn't rely on wildly optimistic growth projections of the sort adopted in the current administration's tax plan. It's instead just a matter of ensuring that such growth as we now have is broadly shared via progressive tax policy and expanded social services. If growth were broadly shared, the pain would be eased, and zero-sum rhetoric would become less attractive. By sharing growth widely, *everyone* at the bottom would benefit, not just those who have lost out recently but also those who have long been oppressed and disadvantaged.

The simplest way to share the country's growth more broadly is to introduce aggressively redistributive tax policy. As Emmanuel Saez and his colleagues have shown, the share of the country's total growth that the poor and middle class are receiving has dramatically declined over the last forty years, a state of affairs that could be instantly corrected with smart tax policy.[15] It will not happen in this administration, but it should be *the* foundational plank of the next.

We are hardly the first commentators to advocate for a social compact founded on a commitment to broadly shared growth. It has not, however, been widely acknowledged that a key benefit of such growth is that it disarms the purveyors of zero-sum politics and internecine conflict. It's the oldest trick in the book to ramp up discontent by keeping income low, making the pain deeply felt, and triggering a search for groups who might then be blamed. We ought not fall for this trick.

The good news here: if we know how to ramp up populism, we also know how to tamp it down. It doesn't require impossibly high rates of economic growth. It doesn't require capitulating to "go-slow advocates" by pulling back on our commitment to reducing discrimination. It doesn't require privileging any group's pain or empathizing with or even understanding that pain. It just requires tried-and-true tax policy that restores our country's longstanding commitment to broadly shared growth.

NOTES

Revised June 23, 2018

1. Although there was, of course, much loss during past recessions, what's unprecedented here is that we've had a protracted period of loss during recessionary and expansionary periods alike. See Raj Chetty et al., "The Fading American Dream: Trends in Absolute Income Mobility Since 1940," *Science* 356, no. 6336 (2017).
2. Chetty et al., "The Fading American Dream."
3. Michelle Jackson and David B. Grusky, "A Post-Liberal Theory of Stratification," *British Journal of Sociology* (October 2018).
4. Jake Rosenfeld, "Little Labor: How Union Decline Is Changing the American Landscape," *Pathways Magazine* (Spring 2010).
5. Jackson and Grusky, "A Post-Liberal Theory of Stratification."
6. Michael Young, *The Rise of the Meritocracy, 1870–2033: An Essay on Education and Equality* (London: Thames & Hudson, 1958).
7. Michael Young, "Down with Meritocracy," *Guardian*, June 28, 2001.
8. Anne Case and Angus Deaton, "Rising Morbidity and Mortality in Midlife Among White Non-Hispanic Americans in the 21st Century," *PNAS* 112, no. 49 (2015).

9. Because estimates of "reverse discrimination" have been quite variable, we would not recommend treating these particular estimates as definitive.

10. Arlie Russell Hochschild, *Strangers in Their Own Land: Anger and Mourning on the American Right* (New York: The New Press, 2016).

11. James Damore, "Google's Ideological Echo Chamber: How Bias Clouds Our Thinking About Diversity and Inclusion" (July 2017), available at https://motherboard.vice.com/en_us/article/evzjww/here-are-the-citations-for-the-anti-diversity-manifesto-circulating-at-google.

12. Quoted in Katy Barnato, "After Trump Speech, WTO Chief Says Protectionist Language Poses Risks to Trade," *CNBC.com*, July 22, 2016, https://www.cnbc.com/2016/07/22/after-trump-speech-wto-chief-says-protectionist-language-poses-risks-to-trade.html.

13. Executive Order no. 13,786, "Omnibus Report on Significant Trade Deficits," March 31, 2017, https://www.whitehouse.gov/the-press-office/2017/03/31/presidential-executive-order-regarding-omnibus-report-significant-trade.

14. James P. Pinkerton, "A Manifesto for the 60 Percent: The Center-Right Populist-Nationalist Coalition," *Breitbart*, September 11, 2016, http://www.breitbart.com/big-government/2016/09/11/manifesto-60-percent-center-right-populist-nationalist-coalition/.

15. Thomas Piketty, Emmanuel Saez, and Gabriel Zucman, "Distributional National Accounts: Methods and Estimates for the United States," *Quarterly Journal of Economics* 133, no. 2 (May 2018). We do not mean to suggest that redistributive tax policy is to be preferred to more fundamental institutional reforms that address predistributional inequalities. It is best viewed as a first step that might then be followed by predistributional reform.

PART III

The Solutions

What We Can Do

WORKING-CLASS ENVIRONMENTALISM

DANIEL ALDANA COHEN

Trump can't make sunlight expensive or slow the wind. He can't make walking more polluting than driving, or energy efficiency more expensive than waste. For all the damage that Scott Pruitt and others are doing to the government's environmental agencies, they can only block so much climate progress. Thanks to a surge of elite and grassroots action countrywide and to market forces shrinking coal use, the U.S. economy might still squeak clear of its Paris carbon-reduction targets.

But Trump's plan can succeed even while failing. The Paris targets aren't ambitious enough for the United States to help forestall climate chaos. The big picture is simple: we need massive, rapid cuts to the emissions of greenhouse gases that cause climate change. (This includes blocking new natural-gas infrastructure.) To get there will require wide popular support and energetic mobilization.

Progressives' and environmentalists' boldest strategy so far has been a work-around: with leadership from former New York City mayor Michael Bloomberg and California governor Jerry Brown, states, tribes, corporations, and hundreds of cities are gathering under the "We Are Still In" umbrella to aggregate their greenhouse-gas-emissions-reduction pledges and collectively meet the country's Paris climate commitments (this is called "America's Pledge"). In November 2017, Bloomberg Philanthropies even paid to get the group a pavilion at the COP23 climate summit in Bonn to represent the "real" America. The Sierra Club joined the fray with its Ready for 100 campaign, where cities commit to using 100 percent renewable energy by 2050.

First, a focus on building regulations is intensely technocratic. It reinforces the false view that you can achieve fast enough progress on climate change through technicians, planners, and financial engineers making uncontroversial improvements to the existing built environment. But far greater changes, demanding more political buy-in, will be needed. Every political psychologist and their mother knows that stories are what move people. But they usually forget the second half of the insight: to work, stories must connect to people's underlying material needs and inspire them at a time when, with housing brutally expensive, health-care costs ever rising, and wages stagnating, economic pain is widespread. The climate story must be shorn of every trace of elitism, of the suspicion that it's a hobby (whether hypocritical or virtuous) for rich people like Bloomberg and Al Gore. Even some of building retrofits' greatest champions can see how awkwardly that policy fits the need for a broad, compelling message.

At a 2017 climate-policy forum in New York City, an audience member asked Mark Chambers, the city's director of sustainability programs, what climate-conscious citizens should be doing. His answer revealed a frustrated longing to transcend his elite policy space: "I want you to recognize the fact that you have an obligation to bring more people into this message," he said. "We cannot keep being this esoteric group of folks that is just tree-huggers and energy wonks that are kind of moving in circles. We have got to recognize that there are millions and millions of people that need us to be able to translate what we're doing into actionable items."

We'll start by deconstructing the method used by countries, regions, and cities in their regular greenhouse-gas-emissions audits: territorial accounting. It works by drawing a border around a jurisdiction and adding up the greenhouse gases emitted within. With cities, one also includes emissions from regional power plants. From this perspective, the policies that progressive mayors are championing—more efficient buildings, more rooftop solar, and tweaked power-purchase agreements—will slash emissions.

But what about the carbon emitted to make the goods and services we consume in cities? Take your smart phone. Territorial accounting only tallies the emissions that result from charging it; it ignores emissions from material mining, manufacturing, and international shipping—your smart phone's "indirect" emissions. The same logic applies to steaks, jeans, and arc lamps—all reliant on polluting activity expelled from the city to operational landscapes far away.

These democratic neighborhoods accidentally became the country's most climate-friendly because for decades, unions, community groups, racial- and environmental-justice organizations, and motivated individuals fought hard to get parks, libraries, sports facilities (even handball and basketball courts), theaters, decent schools, and other low-carbon public amenities installed. These amenities are what foster all the benefits of social connectedness and community; they allow the exchange of meanings to matter more than the exchange of goods even while basic needs are met by decent wages and quality public institutions. (To be clear, it's not because the poor consume so little; they should consume more. The affluent must consume much less.) What made these communities *live* was being anchored by dense housing that residents could afford thanks to public policy. As the urbanist Mike Davis argues, "The cornerstone of the low-carbon city, far more than any particular green design or technology, is the priority given to public affluence over private wealth."

Now, this model of low-carbon urbanism is being threatened by gentrification and displacement. This can shred communities' public life, strip away affordable housing, and—because it often comes with nicer parks and bike lanes—mingle the stories of urban greening and low-carbon urbanism. Gentrification is a huge threat to the low-carbon urban fabric we already have. Now more than ever, urban progressives must cement the alliance between social justice and environmental improvement by vigorously defending affordable housing in dense neighborhoods.

For instance, while 55 percent of city dwellers believe global warming is a very serious issue, only 40 percent of rural Americans (overwhelmingly white) report the same. These numbers must move to enable massive climate action. To bring more white rural workers into a multiracial climate coalition and to deepen the commitment of existing members of that coalition will require fusing climate action with policies that achieve economic fairness.

The federal government has the best tools to do this. It can implement the most comprehensive carbon tax then spend those revenues on rebating consumers, investing on a large scale to accelerate the clean-energy transition, and funding local resiliency projects. It's all about investment. And no one can leverage more money than Washington, DC. (There's no law that limits climate investment to carbon-tax revenue alone.)

As 2020 approaches, bigger states can still step up. Some are trying. Efforts to pass intensely progressive carbon-pricing policies in California and New York gained significant traction despite failing in the summer of 2017; in each case, policies would have dedicated a third or more of revenues to investing in job-rich clean-energy and resiliency projects in racialized and low-income communities. In both states, urban environmental-justice movements were key coalition leaders. There will be time to try again. (California is also leading a push to phase out combustion-engine cars and maintaining a decent cap-and-trade scheme, and, by law, California now dedicates one third of cap-and-trade revenues to investing directly in racialized and working-class communities.)

These projects model an investment-oriented climate politics that prioritizes creating jobs and improving well-being in low-income, working-class, and racialized communities, with governments collaborating with community organizations and social movements. The country's environmental-justice movement has long been a leader in this approach. Their leadership is more important than ever. This is a movement with long experience building novel coalitions around pragmatic, ambitious, and intersectional environmental politics.

The already affluent should help foot the bill. There have been some tentative steps in this direction. New York's mayor, Bill de Blasio, has argued that the city should raise taxes on its wealthiest residents to pay for improvements to the subway system. The labor and community-group coalition Align has begun arguing for more: congestion pricing *and* an extra tax on wealth. (Align is also organizing around what it calls "whole building" retrofits, which do more to bring in social equity.) In support of other public affluence policies, like universal access to preschool, De Blasio has proposed a "mansions tax" and a "millionaires tax." Each time, New York state's governor, Andrew Cuomo, who has himself backed a range of clean-energy policies and exemplifies the centrist current in climate policy making, has slapped down the idea of taxing wealthier New Yorkers.

Most important, to build a broader coalition, city-based climate leaders have to leave the city. For instance, as cities commit to sourcing 100 percent of their energy from renewables, those cities' leaders and social movements can support unionization (and thus high wages and good working conditions) on all projects, and rural, community-based clean-energy projects when the scale makes sense. Urban social movements and political leaders are already supporting campaigns against fossil fuels. Now they need to support rural workers and communities, allowing them to lead in transforming the landscapes where they live. Decarbonizing fast enough to avoid global warming will require massive construction of wind and solar farms and countless miles of new power lines. The climate movement can't afford a rushed, top-down approach that alienates the very people who live where the energy transition must happen.

The idea of rural communities leading this transition is hardly far-fetched. In 2012, roughly half of the clean energy produced in Germany came from community-owned clean-energy cooperatives. Often, these sprung up in conservative villages whose inhabitants just wanted a way to keep local economies moving. There's also the issue of wages. Clean-energy manufacturing usually isn't unionized. Blue-collar workers suffer big wage cuts when they shift to clean energy. Will urban liberals join picket lines and pro-union rallies outside the factories that will build the wind turbines and solar panels that will power our cities? (Rural electricity cooperatives serving tens of millions of consumers are another good place to get active.)

None of these ideas is a panacea. But their underlying principle is simple: slash carbon while fighting inequality. We don't need to wait. To make urban climate politics equitable and to connect to rural workers, progressives and environmentalists should build a commonsense story about climate politics that's based on the best data, that prioritizes economic fairness, and that is tied to immediate action. Urban and rural futures can only be made safe and prosperous together.

NOTE

Revised June 21, 2018.

DEFENDING SOCIETY

WENDY BROWN

Why, today, are many of the most antidemocratic voices in the United States not merely protected by constitutional freedoms but draping themselves in them? Neoliberal political culture, now almost forty years in the making, did not create neofascists, but it did create the conditions in which they represent themselves as freedom fighters, liberating individuals and the nation alike from suffocating laws, policies, and cultural norms imposed by liberals and the Left. Neoliberalism fostered this development through a starkly market-libertarian meaning of freedom, crucially combined with a relentless attack on "the social" and all that it comprises—social powers, social justice, the very idea of a society tended in common. Let us consider the problem of freedom and the attack on the social sequentially before considering the novel antidemocratic form made by their alchemy.

Freedom has many possible permutations. Its neoliberal variant reduces to the absence of coercion, especially by the state but also by anyone or anything with the power to enforce its rules or norms. For Milton Friedman, Friedrich Hayek, and other postwar neoliberal intellectuals, uncoerced action is freedom's only meaning. All other meanings—freedom as emancipation from powers of domination, freedom as capacity, and freedom as participation in popular sovereignty—are simply nonsense from their point of view.

The neoliberal prizing of freedom as noncoercion also goes quite far, challenging a plethora of restrictions on individual or corporate will, including state regulations, taxation, public monopolies, and policies that aim at distributive or social justice. Thus has "freedom" in recent decades become the animating language of tax revolts, challenges to affirmative action, promotion of voucher systems to replace public-school funding, privatization of public goods, and, of course, a series of Supreme Court decisions enhancing the economic and political power of corporations.

A Supreme Court majority schooled in neoliberal jurisprudence and eager to empower conservative and business interests has been especially important to securing this meaning and practice of freedom. As corporations began to rebel against the regulatory and tax state in the late 1970s, they soon found support in a Court quite willing to use the First Amendment as a deregulatory tool on their behalf. Conservative and Christian political movements have also benefited from the Court's willingness to turn the First Amendment into a challenge to equality and antidiscrimination law.

Thus, recent decades have featured a cascade of Court decisions overturning, in the name of freedom, regulations and mandates aimed at securing democracy or social welfare. These decisions have unleashed corporate money in politics (to protect "political speech"); dismantled restrictions on corporate advertising (to protect "commercial speech"); subverted corporate compliance with the contraceptive coverage mandate of the Affordable Care Act (to protect corporate "freedom of conscience"); and permitted escape from antidiscrimination clauses concerning LGBT customers (to protect "religious freedom" and, possibly, in a case yet to be decided, "artistic speech").

As it granted American businesses new powers as "persons" with unqualified First Amendment freedoms, the Court was also busy dismantling worker and consumer solidarities in the name of freedom, upholding "right-to-work" attacks on unions and corporate challenges to class-action law. However, it is not only conflicts between capital and labor or between capital and consumers that are tilted heavily in capital's favor by the antiegalitarian thrust of neoliberal freedom. Equality statutes, health and environmental regulations, gun control, and public goods of every kind have been challenged and overturned by the assertion of rights to be unrestricted by the federal government or social norms.

The power of this stark new form of liberty to dismantle equality and other justice claims was intensified by another plank of the neoliberal revolution, namely its attack on "the social." Famously captured by Margaret Thatcher's 1987 declaration that "there is no such thing as society," only "individual men and women and . . . families," this principle, drawn directly from Hayek, is easily recognized as a challenge to public provisioning and an encomium to individual responsibility. Its meaning and effect went much further, however, and also deeper into the culture, to reject every kind of justice except that delivered by the market.

"The social," Hayek insisted, has no meaning and no place in capitalist orders. For one thing, it was a specious concept, making society into a thing that it wasn't. For another, it was the poison plant from which totalitarianism grew. Social planning, social welfare, social democracy, and of course socialism—all were thrones for coercive state power. All interfered with the productive inequalities of free markets. All replaced the spontaneous order generated by free individuals with dictatorial notions of the Good. Social justice, Hayek claimed, was a "mirage" and, worse, inevitably inverted into its opposite, a totalitarian order dominated by a state unlimited in its juridical and administrative reach.

If Hayek's critique of social justice was iconoclastic in the postwar decades when he was developing it, it has become the common sense of a robust neoliberal conservatism today. In this common sense, the social is the enemy of freedom, and "social-justice warriors" (as today's alt-right calls them) are the enemies of a free people. As neoliberalism became ascendant, this attack on the social—on its very existence and appropriateness as a province of justice—was as consequential as the nakedly libertarian meaning of freedom for building corporate power, legitimating inequality, and unleashing a novel, disinhibited radical-right attack on the most vulnerable members of society.

On the one hand, dismantling the social, and with it concerns with equality apart from formal legal equality and concerns with power apart from explicit coercion, provided this new meaning and practice of freedom with the exclusive mantle of justice. Freedom doesn't simply trump other political principles; it is all there is. On the other, freedom is not just an unlimited right but one exercised without any concern for social context or consequences, without restraint, civility, or care for society as a whole or individuals within it.

Outside of a neoliberal frame, of course, the social is where inequalities are manifest, where subjections, abjections, and exclusions at the site of class, race, and gender are lived, identified, protested, and potentially rectified. As every serious student of inequality knows, the social is a vital domain of justice because it is where the potted histories and hierarchies of a nation are reproduced.

Appreciation of social powers is the only way to understand "taking a knee" or the claim that black lives matter; it is all that explains women's status as working more for less or the high suicide rates among queer teens. Moreover, the social is what binds us in ways that exceed personal ties, market exchange, or abstract citizenship. It is where we, as individuals or a nation, practice or fail to practice justice, decency, civility, and care beyond the codes of market instrumentalism and familialism. And it is where political equality, so essential to democracy, is made or unmade.

Thus the claim that "there is no such thing as society" does far more than challenge social democracy or welfare states as market interference or as creating "dependency" and "entitlement." It does more than propagate the notion that taxes are theft, not the stuff of which civilization is built. It does more than blame the poor for their condition, or the "nature" of blacks, Latinos, and women of all races for their small numbers in elite professions and positions.

Rather, when the claim "society does not exist" becomes common sense, it renders invisible the inequality and social norms generated by legacies of slavery or patriarchy. It permits the effective political disenfranchisement (and not only the suffering) produced by homelessness, lack of education, and health care. Freedom without society destroys the lexicon by which freedom is made democratic, paired with social consciousness, and nested in political equality. It makes liberty a pure instrument of power, shorn of concern for others, the world, or the future.

Reducing freedom to unregulated personal license in the context of disavowing the social and dismantling society achieves something else important. It anoints as free expression every historically and politically generated feeling of (lost) entitlement based in whiteness, maleness, or nativism, and releases it from any connection to social conscience, compromise, or consequence. Lost entitlement to the privileges of whiteness, maleness, and nativism is then easily converted into righteous rage against social inclusion of the historically excluded. This rage in turn becomes the consummate expression of freedom and Americanness. With equality and social solidarity discredited and the existence of powers reproducing historical inequalities, abjections, and exclusions denied, white-male-supremacist politics gain a novel voice and legitimacy in the twenty-first century.

Now we are in a position to grasp how Nazis, Klansmen, and other white nationalists can publically gather in "free-speech rallies," why the authoritarian white male supremacist in the White House is identified with freedom by his supporters through his "political incorrectness," and how decades of policies and principles of social inclusion, antidiscrimination, and racial, sexual, and gender equality come to be tarred as tyrannical norms and rules imposed by "social-justice warriors."

What happens when freedom is reduced to naked assertions of power and entitlement, while the very idea of society is disavowed, equality is disparaged, and democracy is thinned to market meanings? Social justice is demeaned, and crude and provocative expressions of supremacism become expressions of liberty that the First Amendment was ostensibly written to protect. Except it wasn't. It was a promise to democratic citizens to be unmolested by the state in their individual conscience, voice, and faith. It was not a promise to protect vicious attacks on other human beings or groups, any more than it was a promise to submit the nation to a corporatocracy. Alas, a neoliberal culture of unsocial liberty paves the way for both.

What is to be done?

More than ever before, the Left must reckon with the fact that not just the meaning of liberty but its context is protean. Liberty can be detached from democracy and conjoined with other political modalities, including white nationalism, authoritarianism, or plutocracy, which is exactly what is happening today. To ignore this reality, to treat freedom as an unvarying and absolute principle, is to disregard how it can be so severely unmoored from equality that it can turn into open season on the vulnerable.

In this context, we may still want to extend to all the right to speak and assemble. Or we may want to consider that the West's first known democracy, in ancient Athens, did not feature free speech but *isegoria*, equal speech, the right of every citizen to be heard in assemblies concerning public policy. It did not feature freedom from state interference but *isonomia*, equality before the laws of the state. It did not feature managed and bought elections, but *isopoliteia*, equally weighted votes and equal access to political office. Democracy in its cradle was not rooted in individual license but in freedom resting on three pillars of political equality.

If we cannot afford stupidity about how profoundly neoliberalism has stripped freedom of the context and culture that make it an element of justice and popular sovereignty, we also cannot cede freedom to the right, to neoliberalism, and to the white nationalism daily attracting new recruits in the Euro-Atlantic world. Plutocrats, nativists, and fascists have grabbed freedom's mantle to attack democracy, but we cannot fall into the trap of opposing it in the name of other values—security, safety, inclusion, or fairness. Rather, our task is to challenge the neoliberal and right-wing discourse of libertarian and market freedom with a discourse that relinks freedom with emancipation (and thus with social justice) and with democracy (and thus with political equality).

Finally, we must recover a language and a practice of the social for political life and also in our own political work. Left-wing retorts to right-wing speech and policy today too often take the form of demands for protection against personal experiences of injury, fear, or violated rights, which do not repair a lost language of the social but consecrate that loss. A robust language of social power is all that can provide a deep account of the devastating inequalities and the *unfreedom* generated by capitalism along with the legacies of racial and gender subordination. In turn, a language of society is all that can make addressing these inequalities and unfreedoms into a demand on us all, rather than the plaint of interests. A language and practice of society is also essential for binding freedom to equality and to cultivating our world in common.

PROTEST, VIOLENT AND NONVIOLENT

JUDITH BUTLER

Contemporary protests renew debates about whether or not violence is justified, raising questions about what even counts as violence. The demonstrations planned by right-wing groups for late August in Berkeley, to target the teaching of Marxism in universities, were canceled by their organizers and then briefly revived by a small group of people who sought to hold their ground on the lawns adjacent to the city's mayoral offices. A handful arrived with posters praising Trump and objecting to the ostensibly left leanings of the university. They were surrounded by thousands of counterdemonstrators, outnumbered and overwhelmed.

That would have been enough to "demonstrate" that the consensus was clearly against them. But some protestors on the Left decided to harass, chase, and even physically assault their opposition. Their actions attracted media attention, even though they were but a small part of a larger protest that was a deliberately non-violent assembly.

Some claimed that the violence was done by "Antifa"; others named "the Black Bloc" without asking whether these two groups were the same. A calm walk through the crowd fairly quickly made clear that there were those opposed to fascism who were not part of Antifa; Antifa who were against violent tactics, actively practicing nonviolent resistance; and members of the Black Bloc who were not Antifa but working in tentative alliance with them, who in the past have generally targeted property and not persons. There were others who were simply looking for a fight.

Still others were carrying on the love tradition well known in places like Berkeley. Still others thought that more important than opposition to fascism was opposition to racism. Many invoked peace and justice, defining themselves against hate and violence. Most of the love people had already scattered before a few of the counterprotestors decided to beat up on someone apparently distinguished only by the Trump sign he carried. Was their violence planned? If so, how did they justify such an action?

The debate between those who affirm and those who oppose violent tactics has taken on a new form. For some of those who claim that the electoral system brought a fascist to power, it is no longer possible to work within the law. Their reasons are various: the legal electoral process brought fascism to the government and is therefore unjust; the law itself encodes and reproduces the economic violence of capitalism; the law is a tool of the state and so an instrument of state violence that can only be undone through counterviolence.

Under conditions in which the law serves unjust state power or serves an economic system that exercises its own violence, then independent, extralegal judgment and actions are required to oppose state violence. Resistance movements make use of tactics of disobedience and so invariably debate the role of violence. Yet one reason those debates run into difficulty is that it seems as if violence and nonviolence are terms that are already twisted by the frameworks in which they appear: the state can decide to call certain actions "violent" because they are perceived as a threat to its monopoly on violence, even when those actions are nonviolent forms of expression, such as assembly, dissent, boycott, and strike.

On the Left, social structures and systems are regularly called violent even when the structure itself does not physically act but gives rise to forms of subjugation and disenfranchisement that undermine the lives they affect.

In both cases, "violence" is no longer restricted to a physical set of acts. A demonstration can all too easily be called a "riot" when a university administration, a corporation, or a government seeks to justify the use of the army or police or security forces to quell dissent. A "boycott" can be labeled violent even when it is a deliberately nonviolent means of expressing a political objection. Such instances produce confusion about what we are arguing about when we are debating violence.

At one end of the left spectrum are those who rally behind "by any means necessary" (BAMN), by which they mean that all tactics and strategies are justified if they oppose a racist or a fascist regime. And yet would these same people agree to torture, to indefinite detention of their adversary, to political assassination? Elsewhere on that spectrum, however, are many who continue to reference the living tradition of Martin Luther King Jr., who called for and practiced nonviolent protest and distributed leaflets on Gandhi's philosophy at town meetings throughout the South.

These debates refer as well to the oppositional writing of Malcolm X and to Frantz Fanon's "Concerning Violence," although a close consideration of Fanon brings forward arguments both for and against violence at different points in his short career. Even revolutionary and anarchist tracts question whether violence has the power to bring about radical change. Sometimes the arguments against violence are tactical; other times they rest on principle.

For those of us who have taught the debate between violent and nonviolent tactics, a few key examples repeatedly surface. If you defend nonviolence as an unequivocal good, then what would you do if someone attacked a family member—would you not defend that member of your family, even if it meant doing violence to another person? Then there is the question that was posed in my Saturday morning synagogue classes: If the Nazis were on the rise or in power, would you or would you not become part of a resistance movement that included tactics of violence against their institutions, infrastructures, and representatives?

In the synagogue, we all agreed to let our otherwise principled views against nonviolence cede to the exception: we would fight. Fascism seemed and still seems to be the justifiable limit to nonviolence.[1] And yet the fascism we have in mind is Hitler's or Mussolini's. Those historical forms are not exactly the same as the present regime. Even if we can identify fascist strains in this government, does it count as fascism?

Indeed, as that argument enters the contemporary scene, it encounters some difficulties. Contemporary antifascists sometimes argue that there is a continuity between fascism then and now and that we ought not to make the same mistake as people in the 1930s did by failing to recognize its emergence. As a result, they argue, a resistance movement must now include violent tactics, as it did in the righteous struggle against fascists in World War II. Justifying violence on these grounds presumes the continuity or analogy between the two historical instances. But has that been clearly established?

In the last few years, the student movement in South Africa has debated the use of tactics of violence and nonviolence against buildings and infrastructures at the university. Those who affirmed violent tactics made the historical argument that if violence was justified in the overthrow of the legal apartheid, and apartheid now continues to persist in contemporary economic and social forms, especially in the structure of the university, then violence is as justified in dismantling the persistent institutional afterlife of apartheid as it was in taking down the apartheid regime. Once again, is there a strict continuity? Are there, for instance, some black educational institutions that have been built post-apartheid that ought not to be dismantled on such grounds?

Within the contemporary protest movements variously targeting the Trump regime, emergent fascism, state racism, or structural economic inequality, what form do these arguments take? Some would say that Trump is a fascist and has taken steps to produce a fascist regime; others would say that under deregulated and unrestrained forms of capitalism, political resistance must oppose the economic system in its totality: violence is necessary for radical transformation or, indeed, a revolution. Neither Antifa nor the Black Bloc embrace every form of violence (and some of the former remain nonviolent), although presumably those who affiliate with BAMN do not set a limit on justifiable forms of violence as long as they are determined to help realize their goals.

For those who claim that violence is only a provisional tactic or tool, one challenge from a principled position is this: Do we not already know that tools can use their users? The tool of violence is already operating in the world before anyone takes it up; the tool presupposes a world and builds (and unbuilds) a specific kind of world. When we commit acts of violence, we are, in and through the act, building a more violent world.

What might at first seem to be a mere instrument to be discarded when its goal is accomplished turns out to be a praxis, a means that posits an end at the moment it is actualized; the means of violence posits violence as its end. In other words, through making use of violence as a means, one makes the world into a more violent place; one brings more violence into the world. One violence would have to be radically distinguished from another if the violence the left protestors use were to be distinguished from the violence they condemn. But violence, sadly, knows no such distinction.

Violence becomes licensed by both the Left and the Right—and creates for many an even greater estrangement from the political sphere. More than half of eligible voters did not vote in the last election either because of voter suppression, the continuation of Jim Crow that disproportionately disenfranchises black and brown communities, or as a result of pervasive alienation and cynicism about the efficacy of the vote or the representative character of elections. Add to this the nefarious effect of Citizens United, which grants wealthy corporations the right to pour limitless amounts of money into campaigns in the name of a distorted version of "free speech."

A minority elected this government, which means that the electoral result signifies a crisis in democratic politics. Violence only compounds the sense of hopelessness and skepticism about the possibility of practicing democracy, when that is precisely what we need most: the exercise of judgment, freedom, and power within the sphere of politics that can activate the true majority to drive Trump and his crew out of office.

Again, one can argue against violence both on principle and on practical grounds. It is, of course, ironic, if not appalling, that the members of the Black Bloc, a group of mainly white men, emphatically able-bodied, decided to turn the police barricades into instruments of violence and destroyed part of the Martin Luther King Jr. Student Union on the UC Berkeley campus last spring. Did they think in advance about how painful it would be for many people to witness an attack on the building on campus that symbolizes and honors the struggle for civil rights?

Even if one shares the Bloc's passionate opposition to racist and fascist politics, one can question whether they were right to force the cancellation of *Breitbart* editor Milo Yiannopoulos's campus speaking event by producing this scene of violence. And what about their internal gender politics: What form of masculinity is being promoted here? Why are women seen trailing behind their able-bodied men? Is this a new form of antifeminism on the Left?

Nonviolence can be bold and aggressive, even manifest a kind of force. To mobilize now to expand democratic politics, to fight against segregation and white supremacy, we have to think carefully about how best to rally for that purpose. Protest is a way of voting on and with the streets, asserting a sense of the people that remains radically unrepresented by the "representative" government that exists. An assembly outside of the established assemblies, protest establishes the space and time for those disenfranchised to show up and be counted even when, or precisely when, the electoral count has failed them.

Perhaps it is the still vital tradition of Martin Luther King Jr. to whom we should return. King speaks about both radical democracy and nonviolence in his 1967 work, *Where Do We Go from Here?*, which sought to answer the question, *what now?* King understood that violence emerges from a lack of hope and that as it emerges, it further destroys the last remnants of hope: "We maintained the hope while transforming the hate of traditional revolutions into positive nonviolent power. As long as the hope was fulfilled there was little questioning of nonviolence. But when the hopes were blasted, when people came to see that in spite of progress their conditions were still insufferable . . . despair began to set in."

Appalled by an electoral outcome such as this one, we ought to address the radical exclusions that continue to afflict the system that produced this monstrous result. For those who no longer feel represented by politics, or never did, and especially for those forcibly barred from participation, there is profound hopelessness and outrage, and understandably so. The turn to violence, however, further destroys hope and augments the violence of the world, undoing the livable world. The task remains to rally the "we" with the power and desire to build the just and livable world.

NOTE

1. I remember years ago meeting an Auschwitz survivor who had married a man who was a conscientious objector during the Second World War, precisely someone who would not enter the war to save her. I did not at first understand how she could have married him; then I realized that she wanted to marry someone who would never have anything to do with war. That he himself died in an explosion in Lebanon showed that neither of them could fully control that fate.

SOCIAL SOLIDARITY

MICHELE LAMONT

L ike mom and apple pie, football brings Americans together. It enables spectators to participate in collective life loudly and (sometimes) proudly, despite competing team loyalties. Because such moments of unfettered collective effervescence are so rare in the United States, the #TakeAKnee movement is generating strong emotions on all sides of the conflict. To patriotic fans, taking a knee means gross disrespect of the flag. To NFL players, taking a knee means honoring the flag and military while protesting racial police violence and denouncing the broken promises of an American Dream not accessible to all.

Donald Trump, the great divider, is deliberately stoking these tensions. By insulting the protesting players ("sons of bitches"), he panders to his base and flatters the pride of those who wrap themselves in the flag. Yet this collective drama is only the tip of the iceberg: calling out those who "take a knee" is but one episode among many in the great seduction scam Trump has been waging since long before his election, with a white working class as his mark. Promoting a return to wishing "Merry Christmas" is also part of this scam, as is Trump's embrace of "straight" and vulgar talk, which aims to convince folks of his authenticity (coded as antithetical to politically correct middle-class phoniness). And we know there is a scam going on here because so many of his proposed policies, such as the health-care and tax reforms, in actual fact work counter to the interests of workers and foster greater inequality.

Athletes take a knee to defend their wounded dignity and to plead for justice, while Trump's white working-class supporters, long bedeviled by declining living standards and a precarious sense of economic security, seek to reaffirm their place in the world by falling back on the symbols of their national pride and high status (as Americans). They claim recognition through the flag, the national anthem, and, by extension, the military, at the same time as they morally condemn sacrilegious and disloyal Americans, who just happen to be black. Thus the NFL becomes a national cultural battleground for setting the pecking order or for symbolic group positioning. Wounded pride feeds an escalation in racial conflicts at a time when collective trust is at a low point, when "black lives matter" and "all races matter" proponents are sparring with one another in an increasingly schizophrenic public sphere.

Trump claims that his opposition to taking a knee, as too his response to the Puerto Rico hurricane disaster or his border-wall politics or his anti-immigration politics, all have "nothing to do with race." But his disavowal of racism seems half-hearted at best. Too often, the targets of his vitriol are black or brown. In his racially tinged outbursts, he confirms the thesis of Ta-Nehisi Coates that the current president's legitimacy largely hinges on promoting the superiority of whites, and white workers in particular, in defending what they believe is their legitimate group position above all nonwhites.[1]

In a paper titled "Trump's Electoral Speeches and His Appeal to the White Working Class," my coauthors and I draw on a detailed computer-based content analysis of seventy-three of

Trump's electoral speeches to shed light on this seduction scam. We show with numbers that Trump provided this group recognition by blaming globalization for white workers' downward mobility and by stressing their traditional roles as providers and protectors of women and children (against the Muslim threat and Syrian refugees, as well as against Mexican "rapists" and "urban" drug dealers).

We were surprised to discover that prior to being elected, Trump did not explicitly pit white workers against the poor (those who "sponge off the system") but promised "jobs, jobs, jobs" to all hardworking men, in exchange for everlasting loyalty. He also rarely referred to African Americans and Hispanic Americans in explicitly negative language but emphasized how they, too, are victims of a declining American economy. Of course, much of that embrace of blacks and the poor was supplemented with code words—"Detroit" and "Chicago" = poor + black—intended to shore up white stereotypes of these other racial and ethnic groups.

In his electoral speeches, however, Trump did often try to appeal to white workers, underscoring the patriotism of this group by scapegoating immigrants, often lumping legal and illegal immigrants together and feeding the xenophobia nourished by post-9/11 anti-immigrant rhetoric. Focusing on national identity and patriotism, he has found, is a sure way to appeal to downwardly mobile white working men who view Americanness as one of the few badges of honor they still have left in an era in which the material affluence of the American Dream is increasingly out of reach for them. This is particularly the case when their traditional roles as providers and protectors are also being threatened, as women join the labor force in larger numbers.

Trump's seduction scam makes him as popular now among non-college-educated whites as he was right after the election, with

57 percent of them judging that he is doing a good job (the figure for the general population is 37 percent).[2] These numbers are striking when one considers that the main policies that have been under discussion, health-care reform and tax reform, would unambiguously disadvantage this group.

There is something uncanny in how this hate-mongering president systematically and effectively picks tropes that pit groups against one another, accentuating the very markers of class or racial identity that the opposing group will find most repulsive. That he is a marketing genius is not news. But even so, the media have not fully captured how he creates ever-growing havoc in the American polity, feeding hatred and intensifying group boundaries, which translate into an increase in hate speech, bullying in schools, greater social isolation and mental illness, and other standard indicators of a crisis in social solidarity.

In the football drama, the public has continued to be divided. When the NFL required its players to stand during the national anthem in May 2018, only slightly more than half of the American public surveyed did not view taking a knee as unpatriotic[3] (a similar proportion to that in October 2017, when 51 percent of all respondents opposed this symbolic gesture).[4] In his insistence on fostering group hatred by harassing players, could Trump be misreading the situation? Does the popular support for NFL players mark a turning point, as ordinary citizens begin to grasp the game that Trump is playing?

The NFL drama may be teaching us about a way out of the current civic crisis. Social scientists, religious and civic leaders, and journalists and cultural specialists of all stripes have a special role to play in helping citizens develop the tools they need to make sense of the current moment. We have to inform the public about how group hatred is cultivated, about the role of rhetoric and symbols in feeding that hatred, and about intergroup conflict dynamics.

Knowledge workers need to proclaim loud and clear that national pride belongs to everyone and that it takes many shapes and hues. We should also engage in an explicit discussion about how to extend cultural membership to the largest number—white working-class men, the poor, and ethnoracial and religious and sexual minorities alike—through the distribution of resources and by discussing stigmatization (not only racism) and the need to foster solidarity toward all.[5]

The vast racial and class fault lines fissuring our society mean that fewer professionals are in contact with classes other than their own now than was the case just a few decades ago. The growing inaccessibility of higher education feeds this trend as the working class is increasingly relegated to low-quality K–12 and second-tier college education, and this despite important efforts to bring "first-gen" students to top rank universities.

As suggested by UC Hastings law professor Joan Williams, knowledge workers, by becoming blind to the distinctiveness of their own worldview, often lack the compassion and cultural frameworks needed to understand where workers are coming from. Our own short-sightedness deepens the very chasms that Trump exploits.

Finding ways to understand people across these racial and class divides is one of the great challenges of our times. Only by meeting it can we come to mend our social fabric. This will require not only new forms of messaging but also strategizing on how to create bridges in a world of communication that is increasingly organized around echo chambers.

Meeting this challenge will require recommitting to social solidarity and purposefully reflecting on what being middle (or upper-middle) class does to us. Of special difficulty for us in the academy will be to eschew both the political self-satisfaction of progressive/liberal moral rectitude and the privileges of class that many unthinkingly assume to be somehow "deserved." After all, the safe neighborhoods and good schools many academics benefit from are made available to us by rotten taxation and school-financing systems that work at the expense of the majority. Reveling in our privileges and consistently misunderstanding what makes those outside of our socioeconomic enclaves tick (morally and otherwise) enable a certain social myopia that can only serve Trump and his allies.

My book *The Dignity of Working Men* (2000) took a deep dive into the world of its subjects. I found that they were consumed with how to keep the world in moral order and that this motivated many of their political views and the boundaries they drew between various groups ("people above," "people below," the poor, and immigrants). Trump has understood how to tap into their instincts and values. Progressive forces would do well to do the same if they don't want to find themselves facing the prospect, come 2020, of Trump at the helm for four more years.

NOTES

1. Ta-Nehisi Coates, "The First White President," *The Atlantic* (October 2017), https://www.theatlantic.com/magazine/archive/2017/10/the-first-white-president-ta-nehisi-coates/537909/.

2. "U.S. Voters Feel Good About Economy, but Not Trump, Quinnipiac University National Poll Finds; Voters Take a Knee for Both Trump and NFL Players," Quinnipiac University Poll, October 11, 2017, https://poll.qu.edu/national/release-detail?ReleaseID=2491.

3. Max Greenwood, "Poll: Majority Says NFL Players Taking a Knee Isn't Unpatriotic," *The Hill*, June 7, 2018, http://thehill.com/blogs/blog-briefing-room/news/391207-poll-majority-says-nfl-players-taking-a-knee-isnt-unpatriotic.

4. See John Sides, "National Anthem Protests Are Becoming More Popular. You Can Thank Donald Trump," *Monkey Cage* (blog), *Washington Post*, October 25, 2017, https://www.washingtonpost.com/news/monkey-cage

/wp/2017/10/25/national-anthem-protests-are-becoming-more-popular
-you-can-thank-donald-trump/.
5. I developed this argument in the address I recently delivered as president
   of the American Sociological Association (https://vimeo.com/230762647).
   The published version is available here http://journals.sagepub.com/doi
   /abs/10.1177/0003122418773775.

"THE PARLIAMENT OF BODIES"

JACK HALBERSTAM

Since the 1980s and the AIDS crisis, queer communities have fought back against homophobia and transphobia using art and camp cultural production, alongside more conventional forms of political activism. In our present moment of global economic and environmental crisis, we seek new forms of intervention, new articulations of the political project, new ways of finding allies, and new structures of solidarity. This year, the documenta art festival offered one solution.

Just a month before the fateful U.S. elections of 2016, Paul Preciado and the team from documenta convened their first Parliament of Bodies in Athens, Greece. Documenta is a massive and ambitious art show that happens every five years in Kassel, Germany. It stands in direct opposition to the art market and has an explicitly political mission. It was founded in 1955 and first dedicated itself to displaying work by artists whom the Nazis had denounced as "degenerate." With a foundation in antifascist politics and an orientation this year toward queer and transgender art, documenta crafted a response to the onslaught of new forms of right-wing populism and the documentation of Europe's refugee crisis. For the first time it took place in two sites: Kassel, as usual, but also in Athens, Greece—a highly politicized place, especially in the German imaginary, and the site of fierce queer and anarchist opposition to austerity measures. The Parliament of Bodies, which met regularly for one year, staged lectures, performances, activist meetings, and wild and loud discussions. In so doing, it presented a model of how to combat new forms of extreme capitalism and the rise of fascist movements through thought, play, activist interventions, and alternative models of the political.

And then came Trump, as if summoned out of the ashes of utopian dreams. He stood for the rapacious greed of global capitalism and the imminent crisis of environmental decline, on the one hand, and the unmoored orientation of right-wing backlash against refugees, the disintegration of the traditional family, and the rise of economic disparities globally, on the other. Fighting Trumpism, or the consolidation of new forms of fascism that espouse white supremacist policies disguised as economic populism, requires that progressive groups address more than their obvious constituencies and that they find ways to talk to massively exploited but undereducated populations. It also requires that we think beyond the identity politics of an earlier era and recognize the ways in which LGBTQ communities are sometimes targeted but at other times embraced by right-wing politicians seeking a broader base.

The truth—if one can use such a word anymore—about Trump is that there is no unifying principle that defines his approach to the world, to politically hot-button issues, to the economy, to health care, to the politics of sexuality. The only constants are an unremitting orientation to white supremacy, on the one hand, and an undying commitment to protect wealthy corporate interests, on the other. Within these parameters, Trump will say and do anything to enhance his corporate interests and preserve his white identity politics. Accordingly, LGBTQ issues, for Trump, fluctuate depending upon the day of the week, the topic of the hour, and the last person with whom he spoke.

Trump on LGBTQ issues is like Trump on anything—today he is pro-queer; tomorrow he will kick transgender people out of the military; the day after he will endorse gay marriage; and next week he will mention all the great drag queens he knows. This is not policy or the hallmarks of a serious, ideologically committed politician. Instead, it is a mishmash of opinions, personal connections, spontaneous feelings, and clumsy attempts to politically locate himself.

At the Republican convention in July 2016, talking about the Orlando nightclub shootings of forty-nine (mostly gay) men, Trump pledged to "protect our LGBTQ citizens from the violence and oppression of a hateful foreign ideology." The real subject of this sentence, of course, is not actually the protection of LGBTQ people but the defense against "foreign ideology." He used the horrific event as leverage to push his extraordinary notion of a ban on Muslims entering the country.

Candidate Trump also invited Caitlyn Jenner to Trump Tower and told her she could use any bathroom she liked, and he expressed a live-and-let-pee attitude to the question of transgender bathrooms. But then, six months later, in February 2017, the newly inaugurated president, in a clear and not subtle ploy to appeal to part of his conservative base, reversed an Obama-era directive allowing transgender students to use the bathrooms in which they feel most comfortable. Instead, Trump sent the issue back to the states to decide on how to tackle the issue.

In August, Trump announced his intention to ban transgender people from serving in the military, citing the burden of carrying the health-care costs of sex reassignment surgeries as part of his rationale. Again, the initiative seemed to be as much about opposing his predecessor's policy (Obama had opened the way to having transgender people serve openly in the military) as it was about animus toward transgender soldiers.

Trump's flip-flopping set of positions on protections for LGBT people do not fuse into a coherent policy, a clear position, or even an obvious statement of homophobia or transphobia. Trump has no particular stand on LGBTQ issues—if it serves him to offer protection, he will. If it serves him to withdraw protection, he will. If he listens to a gay or transgender friend one day, we will see progress, if he meets with Christian conservatives another day, we will be back to square one. And, as the case of Caitlin Jenner's support of Trump shows, LGBTQ people themselves are not united in their total opposition to Trump. Indeed, by some estimates 14 percent of the LGBTQ population voted for him. While 14 percent might strike some people as a negligible number, that number is likely a very low estimate, given there were surely many stealth votes that went unrecorded by pollsters. The fact that there is a small but wealthy group of gay "Log Cabin Republicans," who vote for their economic interests over any desire to combat homophobia, speaks volumes about the splintering of the queer vote.

In a revealing article in July of this year in the *Washington Post*, the journalists Robert Samuels and Jenna Johnson surveyed the many and contradictory positions that Trump has taken on LGBTQ issues and defined them as "transactional." In addition to the on-again, off-again support/opposition he has shown to transgender youth and transgender soldiers, Samuels and Johnson also list Trump's well-documented friendship with closeted gay attorney Roy Cohn (who makes a heralded appearance in Tony Kushner's *Angels in American* as a bigoted gay man), his support for AIDS funding, and his donations through fund-raising events to AIDS research. In addition, they claim, Trump has offered support in the past for civil protections for LGBTQ people and for gay marriage. And finally, on his TV show, *The Apprentice*, Trump expressed support for gays in the workplace. In fact, on one show in 2005, he recommended hiring gay men because, especially in the fashion and modeling industries, gay men could be counted on not to sexually harass the talent!

Samuels and Johnson report that Trump had a conversation with a gay contestant on *The Apprentice* in which he asked whether the contestant was gay. When the man responded affirmatively, Trump responded with a shrug: "I like steak, someone else likes spaghetti." As we grapple with the analogies here—women are to steak as gay men are to spaghetti—we come to the heart of Trump's position on LGBTQ: it changes as the wind blows and will likely continue to change over the coming years.

Now more than ever, we hope that art can lead us through the political toxic waste and offer imaginative answers to some of our most pressing concerns: environmental ruin, domestic terrorism, racism, police brutality, and political repression. While Hollywood gives us only poor attempts at allegories—*Mother*! But also maybe *It*?—we need to look elsewhere for help in assessing and opposing the politically complex moment we are in. While Trump stands for and was elected in relation to a media-obsessed world in which audiences for even political events want entertainment over substance, we need to rethink the function and form of art and identity.

Returning then to documenta, perhaps there is some hope in the Parliament of Bodies, which described itself as a response to the refugee crisis in Europe, and which, the curators proposed, "revealed the simultaneous failure not only of modern representative democratic institutions but also of ethical practices of hospitality." They continued: "The real Parliament was on the streets, constituted by unrepresented and undocumented bodies resisting austerity measures and xenophobic policies." Notice the way the problem is stated here—the curators do not name fascism per se as the problem but "modern representative democratic institutions"—after all, Brexit was the result of a popular referendum and Trump was democratically elected. When democracy itself is the source of political chaos, they propose, we must look to the many bodies that are neither represented nor counted within democracy: not simply LGBTQ people but "unrepresented and undocumented bodies."

The Parliament of Bodies scheduled events under the title of "exercises of freedom" and created a number of "societies" that were not divided by identitarian missions, but instead were united by their oppositional goals and used the terminology of friendship and affiliation. For example, there included "the Society of Friends of Sotiria Bellou" (developed with AMOQA, Athens Museum of Queer Arts), dedicated to the proliferation of queer and transfeminist politics, and the Cooperativist Society (coordinated with Emanuele Braga and Enric Duran), working on circular economy (or the commitment to recycling and using resources for as long as possible rather than creating mountains of waste) and "communing."

As this list shows, the real work of the real parliament, the parliament of friends, in the streets and in open rebellion against racial capitalism, is ongoing in locations beyond the university, beyond Congress, beyond the museum, beyond traditional media that rushes in to report on and benefit from the latest crisis. We need intellectual experiments such as the Parliament of Bodies if we are to think our way out of this crisis and the ones that will inevitably follow. We need to talk—not just to each other but to and with the random and improvised societies that pass through the parliament of bodies, searching for new forms of being social, doing the political, queering life as we know it. Find your parliament of bodies, convene it, talk, listen, learn, live.

THE RIGHT TYPE OF CITIZENSHIP

JEFFERSON COWIE

The prime problem of our nation," explained Teddy Roosevelt in his 1910 Osawatomie, Kansas, speech on economic nationalism, "is to get the right type of good citizenship." It still is. Working people *want* to pledge their allegiance to a country that will reciprocate with a pledge of allegiance to them. That is the lesson of Trump. A vision of the nation matters.

While many on the cosmopolitan left find visions of national *anything* maudlin—if not downright politically dangerous—the nation-state has long been the main place of redress and identity for most working people. It will continue to be so into the foreseeable future. And if a progressive nationalism—both social and economic—cannot be created, then progressive victories will probably be only short-lived.

The obstacles to such a progressive nationalism begin with the unsubtle and exhausting debate between class and identity politics, a debate in which progressives seem to affirm their frustrating capacity to eat each other alive. After the Trump election, Mark Lilla threw the latest fireball at the divisiveness of identity politics—that is, the building of political positions based on racial, gender, and sexual identities. It is a "largely expressive, not persuasive" form of politics, Lilla argued, one that fixates on the narcissism of difference. It creates a circular firing squad rather than a collective agenda.

Like many others who have made similar arguments before, Lilla faced a storm of criticism, much of which merely expressed the obvious: systemic, state-sponsored discrimination based on racial, gender, and cultural categories still thrives in this country. And we have an unholy amount of dismantling to get through before we can begin to talk about a post-identity-politics agenda. Both critiques are correct in their analyses and wrong in their politics.

Those, like Lilla, who posit the New Deal and postwar era as an antediluvian time of "pre–identity politics," when collective economic interests could reign supreme, miss some important and troubling history. The problem is, identity and class do not make up a tidy binary.

The most divisive and tribal issues in American politics today—race, immigration, sexual identity, and the culture wars—functioned completely differently in the postwar era from how they did before the war or after the 1960s. The New Deal excluded protections for predominantly African American occupations, such as agriculture and service work, keeping such laborers outside of social security, collective bargaining, and fair labor standards, in order to preserve the unholy alliance with Southern Democrats that Northern progressives needed to pass their cherished reforms.

Large-scale immigration was largely shut down with the imposition of the quota system in 1924 and did not really open again until 1965. This meant that during the New Deal and the decades following there was no new immigrant population large enough to prove politically polarizing. Furthermore, the post–World War II era is seen by religious scholars as a time of "religious truce," during which a vague new invention called

"Judeo-Christian values" stood up to the international threat of atheistic communism.

The point is, once you factor out—by hook or by crook—the persistent pressures of social, ethnic, and cultural heterogeneity in American politics, it becomes a lot easier to pass policies that begin to look like a modest version of social democracy in America. It is a truism of political science that social democracy flourishes best among homogenous populations, and the realm of postwar American politics was more homogeneous than the period before the 1930s or after the 1970s. So a blinkered version of "class" politics worked. Glory Days it was, at least for white, male industrial workers, as I argue in *The Great Exception: The New Deal and the Limits of American Politics* (2016).

But here's the thing: in that New Deal golden age for white, male industrial workers, wages were going up not just for those steel and auto workers but for men and women of *all races and almost all regions*. The "spillover effect" of economic security even beyond the organized, basic industries proved dramatic, national in scope, and multifaceted.

Also going up were hope, opportunity, political generosity, and the idea that hard work might just pay off, which in turn created some space for what we might term "progress" in race relations. For all the real racial hate unleashed in America after the Supreme Court's landmark *Brown v. Board of Education* (1954) decision, in the mid-1960s the Civil Rights Act and the Voting Rights Acts *did* actually pass, with enormous long-term implications for social justice in the country.

When the new social movements of the 1960s levied their claims for greater inclusion and equity, they were buoyed and supported by—indeed they *presumed*—a world in which capitalism worked better than it had before. It certainly worked better than the kleptocracy we have today. Although those social movements quickly turned to frustrated indictments of "Amerika" and then had to fight the narrowing horizons brought on by 1970s stagflation, their very existence nonetheless suggests that the postwar political climate from which they emerged was more enriching than its caricature as a simple *herrenvolk* democracy. The potential exists for something more than a race-based vision of community.

At the same time, critics like Lilla, Todd Gitlin, Walter Benn Michaels, and Adolph Reed are right to castigate the politics of "identity" and "diversity" as handmaidens of neoliberal capitalism. Even perfectly equitable access cannot be called success when the system itself is failing: look, we can all have equal access to lousy, criminally overpriced health care! We can all be exploited in precarious jobs with equal treatment! Even when gilded with a commitment to diversity, American inequality is a national failure. In this light, the conflict between identity and class politics appears much less a political-philosophical binary than a messy historical problem.

Bayard Rustin, a gay black man who was the tactical genius behind the Civil Rights Movement, saw this clearly in the mid-1960s. Rustin believed that the best hope for the Civil Rights Movement at the time was to move from protest to real political power that could address policy and economic questions. He knew that the politics of institutions win while the politics of outrage drift off into the wind and require ever more gusts of outrage to keep the sails of condemnation full. In his classic 1965 essay, "From Protest to Politics," Rustin dismissed as counterproductive the easy and distracting project of exposing white liberals for their hypocrisy. Moral outrage, he believed, was not politics; the only thing that truly mattered was *political power*. And the only way to gain political power was to have allies—lots of them.

"The future of the Negro struggle," he wrote, "depends on whether the contradictions of this society can be resolved by a coalition of progressive forces which becomes the effective political majority in the United States. I speak of the coalition which staged the March on Washington, passed the Civil Rights Act, and laid the basis for the Johnson landslide—Negroes, trade unionists, liberals, and religious groups." The saddest thing that happened to the freedom struggle was that antiracism became an abstract goal, stripped of the economic citizenship and party politics that mattered so much to the elders of the civil rights generation.

Like Rustin, the philosopher Nancy Fraser already has a lot of this figured out. Asked to choose between class and identity politics, one must simply reject the question outright, she argues. "Justice today requires both redistribution and recognition. Neither alone is sufficient." No recognition without redistribution, no redistribution without recognition. And, as Fraser does, we might add that none of this works without *participation* in the real ugliness of actual party politics.

Regrettably, however, the selling out of the country to a transnational corporate elite has been a bipartisan effort. But the Republicans do it with God and flag in hand; the Democrats, waving a limp idea of "diversity"; and the results are clear. In 2016, Trump won claiming that he would "Make America Great Again," with nothing but hot air for policy. Hillary Clinton lost with a vapid, vaguely feminist slogan, "I'm with Her" and a laundry list of smart policies. It's an old story. Jimmy Carter lost because he said there was a "crisis of confidence"; Reagan won because he believed in national greatness. Time and again, the language of national vision wins out.

Perhaps the most telling legend is this: one of Ronald Reagan's aides, having watched his candidate offer a full-throated paean to national greatness in 1984, is said to have remarked, "I feel sorry for Mondale, he has to run against America." This is an unwinnable contest: the construct known as America will always prevail.

Like Reagan before him, Trump throws into stark relief just what the Democrats should have taken up in their turn to the right: not the policies that foster greater inequality, but *a vision of national citizenship.*

In contrast, anyone who has traveled the heartland in the last twenty years knows that the words "NAFTA" and "Clinton" still symbolize the Democratic Party's national sellout for many working-class voters. Democratic support for such neoliberal policies took off in the late 1980s and early 1990s, when the Democratic Leadership Council decided to push the party to the right in order to compete on the new terrain created by the Reagan landslide. By giving the party over to corporate power and severing ties with rank-and-file voters in favor of big-money donors, the DLC switch meant playing on the other team's field rather than updating its own. While this delivered short-term victories during the Clinton years, ultimately it undermined the party's connection to its "base" and paved the way for reaction.

The lesson of the Trump election is not that the white working class is too fixated on resenting identitarian movements to ever embrace progressive politics. Working people, even members of the white working class, can and will be progressive if they aren't anxious that "progress" will itself be distributed according to identity categories, gracing everyone other than them. On the other hand, the politics of class qua class are a long way off from reality, and the labor movement is not going to come rushing in to save the day. We need to change the battlefield of the culture wars from who is in and who is out to *we're in this together.*

The country is starved for a meaningful politics of what it means to be an American. Without it, working people are left to bear the local burdens of a cosmopolitan elite who have essentially seceded from the American project. Voting is often irrational, based on vague feelings and gut impulses. The voices of progress need to give people a meaningful national impulse, not a seventeen-point plan on a website or righteous indignation that can be exploited by the likes of Steve Bannon to charge up the right.

Changing the playing field from a limited us-versus-them terrain to the United States of America as a whole is not easy. And it's certainly not the most politically correct or ideologically pure approach. But in the great tradition of American pragmatism, it is the one that can work.

The pragmatist philosopher Richard Rorty pushed for such a vision of national meaning in *Achieving Our Country*, based largely on his readings of Walt Whitman and John Dewey. Without the conscious creation rather than the mere assertion of solidarity, there can be no progress. And the unifying theme of that creative process needs to be, in the midst of globalization and destabilization, a nationalism that can honestly unite across class and identity, that can make inroads into the right's popularity, that can take charge of the global Brexit mood, and that can challenge the power of the corporation over the American citizenry.

If that does not happen, if the alienating and debilitating politics of otherness continues, well, Rorty nailed that, too. After the Trump victory, his prediction, made in 1998, of what happens without a positive national vision, went viral:

> Members of labor unions, and unorganized unskilled workers, will sooner or later realize that their government is not even trying to prevent wages from sinking or to prevent jobs from being exported. Around the same time, they will realize that suburban white-collar workers—themselves desperately afraid of being downsized—are not going to let themselves be taxed to provide social benefits for anyone else.
>
> At that point, something will crack. The nonsuburban electorate will decide that the system has failed and start looking

around for a strongman to vote for—someone willing to assure them that, once he is elected, the smug bureaucrats, tricky lawyers, overpaid bond salesmen, and postmodernist professors will no longer be calling the shots. . . . Once such a strongman takes office, nobody can predict what will happen.[1]

Dissenting movements today are reminiscent of James Baldwin's criticism of the stridency of the American protest novel: "a mirror of our confusion, dishonesty, panic, trapped and immobilized in the sunlit prison of the American dream."[2] Dark forces are ready to move on that prison if enlightened ones do not.

Screws have been turning on the American working class for well over a generation now. In fact, for the bottom quintile of the employed population, real wages peaked during the Nixon administration. Expectations are low and anger is high. Both the moral outrage in the streets and the technocratic neoliberalism in Democratic Party headquarters are traps. The way forward, the way to build a cross-class alliance that can include the working-class vote—a vote made up not only of white guys but of a full mosaic of racial, gender, and cultural complexity—is to look toward a compelling progressive vision for the nation.

Nationalism is dangerous stuff in places with a history of settler colonialism and territorial expansion like the United States, but Lincoln pulled it off. So did Eugene Debs. And both Roosevelts, too. Obama returned to Osawatomie in 2011, as the nation continued to struggle with the financial meltdown, and tried to rekindle Teddy Roosevelt's ghost. Expressing his "deep conviction that we're greater together than we are on our own," he declared that unity and sharing are "American values. And we have to reclaim them." Since then, Bernie Sanders tried to put some policy meat on the bones, but his criticism of corporate power lacked the sense of national "rendezvous with destiny" so artfully invoked by both FDR and Ronald Reagan.

While the follow-through on Obama's Osawatomie speech proved inadequate for a number of reasons, the idea was right. Until we find a social patriotism that works—a path to citizenship for immigrants, a model of economic citizenship for workers, an innovative form of environmental citizenship, an inclusive citizenship for all peoples of all types—then we'll remain vulnerable to the sterile sense of purpose offered by neoliberal individualism or the barbarism of dangerously cartoonish strongmen who can divide but cannot lead.

NOTES

1. Richard Rorty, *Achieving Our Country: Leftist Thought in Twentieth-Century America* (Cambridge, MA: Harvard University Press, 1998), 89–90.
2. James Baldwin, "Everybody's Protest Novel," in *The Price of the Ticket: Collected Nonfiction, 1948–1985* (New York: St. Martin's, 1985), 31.

MULTIRACIAL COOPERATION

WILLIAM JULIUS WILSON

During periods when people are beset with economic anxiety, they become more receptive to political messages that deflect attention away from the real and complex sources of their problems. To counter this tendency, it is vitally important that political leaders channel citizens' frustrations in positive, constructive directions. Unfortunately, in the past year and a half a mean-spirited and divisive rhetoric has instead been on dramatic display in the United States as Donald Trump and his surrogates exaggerate the "dangers" of immigration and the need to "build a wall" between the United States and Mexico to curtail illegal crossings. In various speeches Trump has maintained that Mexican immigrants "compete directly against vulnerable American workers," that they are "rapists," and that they are "bringing drugs" and "bringing crime" to America. These contentious messages and related negative narratives about the behavior and traits of people of color seem to resonate with segments of the white population, especially those who are struggling.

Reflecting on studies that might shed some light on these developments, the social scientist Carol Graham deduced: "In the 2016 elections in the United States it was those cohorts who either have experienced downward mobility or fear it who supported a candidate proposing to build a wall, ban trade, and further divide society along racial and other lines."[1]

Graham's assertion was in part based on her analysis of Gallup Healthway's national survey data from 2008 to 2013, which revealed that poor whites were the most pessimistic group in America about their future.[2] A 2011 survey by the Pew Charitable Trusts' Economic Mobility Project came to a similar conclusion in terms of non-college-educated whites.[3] A majority of them reported that they didn't expect their economic situation to improve in the next ten years, and 43 percent said that they weren't better off than their parents were at the same age; also, only one-third believed their children will live better lives than they do.

No other group in the survey—neither blacks, nor Hispanics, nor educated whites—reported such gloomy outlooks. Other research reveals that non-Hispanic white men and women with only a high school degree or less are experiencing marked declines in life expectancy due to increasing death rates from drug and alcohol poisonings, chronic liver diseases, cirrhosis, and suicide.[4]

More recently, an empirical basis for directly relating economic and physical well-being to political support for Donald Trump has been provided by Jonathan Rothwell and Pablo Diego-Rosell's analysis of Gallup Daily Tracking survey microdata from July 2015 to October 2016, which included over 125,000 interviews.[5] Although their results do not neatly link support for Trump with social and economic hardship, the data do clearly reveal that Trump supporters are more likely to reside in white, segregated enclaves with few college graduates, higher reliance on social security, higher rates of disability and middle-age mortality, and lower rates of intergenerational mobility.[6] These findings lend support to the view that economic anxiety and distress among working-class or downwardly mobile middle-class white Americans are positively associated with political support for Donald Trump.

While Trump's divisive populist messages seem to resonate with working-class whites, the voices of progressives, who are more likely to associate the problems of these citizens with complex changes in our global economy and with failed economic and social policies, seemed—with the notable exception of the Bernie Sanders campaign, which I will discuss below—to fade into the background and have hardly undercut the prevailing mean-spirited rhetoric.

In previous years, I was hopeful that a constructive dialogue would emerge on how problems of ordinary Americans can be addressed in an era of rising inequality.[7] I highlighted concerns that the poor, working and middle classes of all groups share—including concerns about declining real wages, job security and unemployment, escalating medical and housing costs, the availability of affordable childcare programs, and pensions or retirement security. I also argued that programs created in response to these concerns, despite being race-neutral, would disproportionately benefit the inner-city poor but they would also benefit large segments of the remaining population, including the white population.

I also pointed out that national opinion polls in the United States suggest that careful framing of issues to address the problems of ordinary Americans could enhance the possibility of a new alignment in support of major social-rights initiatives, such as universal health care or childcare subsidies for working parents or affordable higher education. If such an alignment is attempted, I reasoned, it ought to highlight a new public rhetoric that focuses on and addresses the problems of all groups, a public rhetoric that would accompany attempts to mobilize these groups through coalition politics. I stated that the framers of this message should be cognizant of the fact that "these groups, although often seen as adversaries, are potential allies in a reform coalition because they suffer from a common problem: economic distress caused by forces outside of their control."[8]

This argument is being repeated by some observers in the U.S. postelection analysis and debates, including those who maintain that the Democrats' emphasis on identity politics—in attempts to mobilize people of color, women, immigrants, and the LGBT community—tended to ignore the problems of poorer white Americans.[9] One notable exception, they point out, was Bernie Sanders's progressive and unifying populist economic message in the Democratic primaries, a message that resonated with a significant segment of the white lower- and working-class populations. However, Sanders was not the Democratic nominee, and Donald Trump was able to capture notable support from these populations with a divisive, not unifying, populist message.

The racial divide in America reduces the political effectiveness of ordinary citizens. That said, multiracial political cooperation could be enhanced if different groups focused more on the interests that their individual members hold in common, such as addressing economic insecurity resulting from political and economic forces beyond their control, and if they could develop a sense of interdependence.

Social-psychological research on interdependence reveals that when people believe that they need each other they tend to relinquish their initial prejudices and stereotypes and are able to join in programs that foster mutual interaction and cooperation. Moreover, when people from different groups do get along, their perceptions about and behavior toward each other undergo change.[10] Under such circumstances, not only do the participants in the research experiment try to behave in ways that do not disrupt the interaction, but they also, when confronted with a given issue, make an effort to express opinions similar to those of others in the experiment.

This research suggests that factors promoting perceived interdependence include, first of all, making individuals and groups aware of common interests, norms, values, aspirations, and goals and then helping them appreciate the importance of interracial cooperation to achieve them. So the basic theoretical argument is the following: A necessary condition for the development of multiracial cooperation is perceived interdependence among potential participants, whereby members of a particular group come to recognize that they cannot achieve their common goals without the help of members of other groups. Visionary group leaders, especially those who head strong community organizations, are essential for articulating and communicating this vision, as well as for developing and sustaining this multiracial political coalition.

In the age of Donald Trump a situation may have been created, at least temporarily, wherein the framing of issues to identify and promote a common goal in coalition building is, perhaps paradoxically, actually less challenging. For example, a May 4 article in the *Washington Post* entitled "Turning Away from Street Protests, Black Lives Matter Tries a New Tactic in the Age of Trump," stated that because of the election of Donald Trump, Black Lives Matter activists feel that they now have to enter a new phase, one that focuses more on politics than on protests. Based on interviews with more than a half a dozen leaders of the Black Lives Matter movement, the article reported that the election of Donald Trump has led them to shift their focus from street protest to joining others in a political coalition that would amass "electoral power to fight an administration that has pledged to roll back Obama-era efforts to reshape policing practice."[11]

Another indication of the potential for such a coalition in the age of Trump is the successful grassroots organizing against the Republican-drafted health-care bill by groups such as the Center for Community Change, the West Virginia Healthy Kids and

Families Coalition, and the Progressive Leadership Alliance of Nevada. The efforts of these multiracial coalitions, including their organizing in white working-class and rural communities, have resulted in a "sea shift in the underlying politics of health care."[12]

These two developments suggest that conditions may now be particularly conducive for launching a progressive national multiracial political coalition not only to bring down the Trump administration but to overcome the congressional gridlock that handcuffed Barack Obama. I would hope that potential members of this coalition (grassroots community organizations, civil rights groups, women's rights groups, labor unions, and religious organizations) would recognize the true task before us, and begin developing interconnected local, regional, and national networks to enhance feelings of perceived interdependence, and thereby reduce racial and ethnic antagonisms, in the pursuit of highly valued common goals.

NOTES

1. Carol Graham, *Happiness for All? Unequal Hopes and Lives in Pursuit of the American Dream* (Princeton, NJ: Princeton University Press, 2017), 101.
2. Graham, *Happiness for All?*, 93.
3. Cited in Ronald Brownstein, "The White Working Class: The Most Pessimistic Group in America," *Atlantic*, May 27, 2011, https://www.theatlantic.com/politics/archive/2011/05/the-white-working-class-the-most-pessimistic-group-in-america/239584/.
4. Anne Case and Agnus Deaton, "Rising Morbidity and Mortality in Midlife Among White Non-Hispanic Americans in the 21st Century," *Proceedings of the National Academy of Sciences of the United States of America* 112, no. 49 (2015), http://www.pnas.org/content/112/49/15078.full.
5. Jonathan Rothwell and Pablo Diego-Rossell, "Explaining Nationalist Political Views: The Case of Donald Trump," November 2, 2016, https://papers.ssrn.com/sol3/papers.cfm?abstract_id=2822059.
6. Rothwell and Pablo Diego-Rossell, "Explaining Nationalist Political Views."

7. See William Julius Wilson, *When Work Disappears: The World of the New Urban Poor* (New York: Knopf, 1996); and *The Bridge Over the Racial Divide: Rising Inequality and Coalition Politics* (Berkeley: University of California Press and the Russell Sage Foundation, 1999).

8. Wilson, *The Bridge over the Racial Divide*, 43.

9. See, for example, Mark Lilla, "The End of Identity Liberalism," *New York Times*, November 18, 2016, https://www.nytimes.com/2016/11/20/opinion /sunday/the-end-of-identity-liberalism.html.

10. For good discussions of this research see Susan T. Fiske, "Stereotyping, Prejudice, and Discrimination," *The Handbook of Social Psychology*, 4th ed., edited by Daniel T. Gilbert, Fiske, and Gardner Lindzey (New York: McGraw Hill, 1998),;and David W. Johnson, Roger Johnson, and Geoffrey Maruyama, "Goal Interdependence and Interpersonal Attraction in Heterogeneous Classrooms: A Meta-Analysis," in *Groups in Contact: The Psychology of Desegregation*, edited by Norman S. Miller and Marilynn B. Brewer (Atlantic Highlands, NJ: Academic Press, 1984).

11. Janell Ross and Wesley Lowery, "Turning Away from Street Protests, Black Lives Matter Tries a New Tactic in the Age of Trump," *Washington Post*, May 4, 2017, https://www.washingtonpost.com/national/in-trumps -america-black-lives-matter-shifts-from-protests-to-policy/2017/05/04 /a2acf37a-28fe-11e7-b605-33413c691853_story.html.

12. Center for Community Change, "At the Center: CCC Quarterly Newsletter," August 3, 2017, https://www.communitychange.org/at-the-center -newsletter-summer-2017/.

CONTRIBUTORS

MICHELLE WILDE ANDERSON is a professor of property, local government, and environmental justice at Stanford Law School. She is currently writing a book about the fight to save basic public services in high-poverty, postindustrial areas. Her work has appeared in the *New York Times*, the *Los Angeles Times*, the *Chicago Tribune*, the *Yale Law Journal*, and other publications.

GRETCHEN BAKKE holds a PhD from the University of Chicago in cultural anthropology. Her work focuses on the chaos and creativity that emerge during social, cultural, and technological transitions. For the past decade she has been researching and writing about the changing culture of electricity in the United States. She is currently a visiting professor at the Institute for European Ethnology at Humboldt University in Berlin. Her book *The Grid* was selected by Bill Gates as one of his top five reads of 2016.

WENDY BROWN is Class of 1936 First Chair at the University of California, Berkeley, where she teaches political theory. A 2017–18 Guggenheim Fellow, her most recent book is *Undoing the Demos: Neoliberalism's Stealth Revolution* (2015). She is currently completing a book on the novel hard-right formation fashioned by neoliberal libertarianism, moral traditionalism, and authoritarian statism.

JUDITH BUTLER is Maxine Elliot Professor in the department of comparative literature and critical theory at the University of California, Berkeley. She is the author of *Notes Toward a Performative Theory of Assembly* (2015).

CRAIG CALHOUN is president of the Berggruen Institute. He was previously director of the London School of Economics and Political Science and before that president of the Social Science Research Council. His books include *Does Capitalism Have a Future?* (2013), *The Roots of Radicalism* (2012), and *Nations Matter* (2007).

DANIEL ALDANA COHEN is assistant professor of sociology at the University of Pennsylvania, where he directs the Socio-Spatial Climate Collaborative, or (SC)2. His writing on climate change, cities, and politics has appeared in *Nature, Public Culture, Metropolitics, Jacobin, Dissent, Public Books,* and elsewhere.

JEFFERSON COWIE is the author of *Stayin' Alive: The 1970s and the Last Days of the Working Class* (2010) and *The Great Exception: The New Deal and the Limits of American Politics* (2016). He holds the James G. Stahlman Chair of American History at Vanderbilt University.

ALINA DAS is an immigrant-rights professor, attorney, and activist. She is a professor of clinical law at New York University School of Law, where she codirects the Immigrant Rights Clinic. She litigates and writes in the area of deportation and detention defense on behalf of immigrant communities.

ASHLEY FARMER is an assistant professor of history and African and African diaspora studies at the University of Texas–Austin. She is a graduate of Spelman College and holds a PhD in African American studies and an MA in history from Harvard University. Her book *Remaking Black Power: How Black Women Transformed an Era* (2017) is the first comprehensive intellectual and social history of black women in the movement.

LINDA GORDON is a university professor of the humanities and the Florence Kelley Professor of History at New York University.

She is the author of several books, including, most recently, *Dorothea Lange: A Life Beyond Limits* (2009) and *Feminism Unfinished* (2014).

PHILIP GORSKI is professor of sociology and religious studies at Yale University, where he is currently concluding a major project on the philosophy of the social sciences. His most recent book is *American Covenant: A History of Civil Religion from the Puritans to the Present* (2017).

DAVID B. GRUSKY is Barbara Kimball Browning Professor in the School of Humanities and Sciences, professor of sociology, director of the Stanford Center on Poverty and Inequality, and coeditor of *Pathways Magazine*. His research addresses the dynamics of late-industrial poverty, inequality, and mobility.

JACK HALBERSTAM is professor of English and gender studies at Columbia University. Halberstam is the author of six books, mostly recently *Trans*: A Quick and Quirky Account of Gender Variance* (2017). Halberstam blogs at bullybloggers.com about popular culture and queer theory and is currently finishing a book titled *Wild Things: Queer Theory After Nature*.

OONA A. HATHAWAY is a professor at Yale Law School and coauthor of *The Internationalists: How a Radical Plan to Outlaw War Remade the World* (2017).

MICHELLE JACKSON is an assistant professor of sociology at Stanford University. Her research examines the power and persistence of socioeconomic background in shaping life chances in late-industrial societies.

SHAMUS KHAN is professor and chair of sociology at Columbia University and the editor of *Public Culture*.

MICHÈLE LAMONT is professor of sociology and African American studies at Harvard; director, Weatherhead Center for International Affairs; and codirector, Successful Societies Program, Canadian Institute for Advanced Research. She is the past president of the American Sociological Association and the 2017 recipient of the prestigious Erasmus Prize.

MARGARET LEVI, Stanford University, is the Sara Miller McCune Director of the Center for Advanced Study in the Behavioral Sciences, a professor of political science, and a senior fellow of the Woods Institute for the Environment. She is the Jere L. Bacharach Professor Emerita of International Studies and the Harry Bridges Chair Emerita at the University of Washington. She is a fellow of the National Academy of Sciences, the American Academy of Arts and Sciences, the John Simon Guggenheim Foundation, and the American Academy of Political and Social Sciences. She served as president of the American Political Science Association from 2004 to 2005. In 2014 she received the William H. Riker Prize in Political Science and in 2017 gave the Elinor Ostrom Memorial Lecture. Her most recent book is *In the Interest of Others* (with John Ahlquist).

TANYA MARIE LUHRMANN is the Watkins University Professor at Stanford University. Her work has been featured in the *New York Times*, the *New Yorker*, the *New York Review of Books*, and many other publications. She is the author of *When God Talks Back: Understanding the American Evangelical Relationship with God* (2012).

STEVEN LUKES is professor of sociology at NYU. His books include *Emile Durkheim: His Life and Work*; *Power: A Radical View*; *Moral Relativism*; and *The Curious Enlightenment of Professor Caritat: A Comedy of Ideas*. His writings and teaching range across political sociology, political theory, and the philosophy of the social sciences.

DOUGLAS S. MASSEY is the Henry G. Bryant Professor of Sociology and Public Affairs at Princeton University and director of its Office of Population Research. He regularly teaches a course entitled Race and Public Policy at Princeton's Woodrow Wilson School of Public and International Affairs.

PEDRO NOGUERA is a distinguished professor of education at the Graduate School of Education and Information Studies at UCLA. His research focuses on the ways in which schools are influenced by social and economic conditions, as well as by demographic trends in local, regional, and global contexts. He is the author of 12 books and over 200 articles and monographs.

VICTOR PICKARD is an associate professor at the Annenberg School for Communication at the University of Pennsylvania. He is the editor (with Robert McChesney) of *Will the Last Reporter Please Turn Out the Lights* and the author of *America's Battle for Media Democracy: The Triumph of Corporate Libertarianism and the Future of Media Reform* (2014).

SASKIA SASSEN is the Robert S. Lynd Professor of Sociology at Columbia University, where she also cochairs the Committee on Global Thought. Her books have been translated into twenty-one languages and include, most recently, *A Sociology of Globalization* (2007); *Territory, Authority, Rights: From Medieval to Global Assemblages* (2008); and the fourth, fully updated edition of *Cities in a World Economy* (2011).

RICHARD SENNETT writes about cities, labor, and culture. He teaches sociology at New York University and at the London School of Economics.

HAREL SHAPIRA is an ethnographer and assistant professor in the Department of Sociology at the University of Texas at Austin. He is the author of *Waiting for José: The Minutemen's Pursuit of America* (2013).

SCOTT J. SHAPIRO is a professor at Yale Law School and coauthor of *The Internationalists: How a Radical Plan to Outlaw War Remade the World* (2017).

PATRICK SHARKEY is the author of *Uneasy Peace: The Great Crime Decline, the Renewal of City Life, and the Next War on Violence*, published by W. W. Norton in January 2018. He is professor and chair of sociology at NYU and is affiliated with NYU's Wagner School for Public Service and Crime Lab New York.

ROBERT M. SHRUM is the Carmen H. and Louis Warschaw Chair in Practical Politics at the University of Southern California and author of *No Excuses: Concessions of a Serial Campaigner*

(2007). A longtime political consultant, he was senior strategist in the presidential campaigns of Al Gore (2000) and John Kerry (2004). He is also the director of the Institute of Politics at USC.

THOMAS J. SUGRUE is the professor of social and cultural analysis and history at NYU and the director of the NYU Collaborative on Global Urbanism. His books include the Bancroft Prize–winning history of Detroit, *The Origins of the Urban Crisis*, and, most recently, with Domenic Vitiello, *Immigration and Metropolitan Revitalization in the United States*.

FRED TURNER is Harry and Norman Chandler Professor of Communication at Stanford University. He is the author, most recently, of *The Democratic Surround: Multimedia and American Liberalism from World War II to the Psychedelic Sixties* (2013).

LISA WADE is a professor of sociology at Occidental College. In addition to dozens of research papers, chapters, and essays, she is the coauthor of *Gender: Ideas, Interactions, Institutions* (2015); coeditor of *Assigned: Life with Gender* (2017); and the author of a book about the culture of sex on campus, *American Hookup* (2017).

WILLIAM JULIUS WILSON is Geyser University Professor at Harvard. A recipient of the 1998 National Medal of Science, the highest scientific honor bestowed in the United States, his many publications include three award-winning books—*The Declining Significance of Race* (1978, 1980, 2012), *The Truly Disadvantaged* (1987, 2012), and *When Work Disappears* (1996).